ANOTHER CUP OF TEA

Diary of a dementia carer

MARTIN DEWHURST

Another Cup of Tea

First published in 2020 by

Panoma Press Ltd
48 St Vincent Drive, St Albans, Herts, AL1 5SJ, UK
info@panomapress.com
www.panomapress.com

Book layout by Neil Coe.

978-1-784529-09-3

Dedication

Dedicated to a loving Mum

Lillian 'Joan' Dewhurst

1st April 1927 – 18th October 2019

Acknowledgements

To Mum and Dad. To my partner Carol. To my children Owen and Alex.

To brother Robin, sister-in-law Jan and their children Beth and Josh. To David and Eileen. To family, friends and neighbours who called on Mum throughout her illness. To Jeanie and Peter.

To Edie and the wonderful team of staff and nurses at Macclesfield General Hospital. To Belinda.

To the carers from Helping Hands and Carers Trust.

To Mindy, Elaine, Tracy, Chris, Mark and Babs. To Elaine. To Ken. To Susan and all the staff at Woodlands Care Home.

And finally, to all who've helped bring this diary to life.

Foreword

In the final stages of his bringing this book to life, I shared a message of support with Martin. It was an honest reflection on what I had been privileged to observe from the sidelines, and through many conversations with Martin, as he cared for and loved his mum along her fog-bound journey to that distant horizon and shores unknown where a new dawn awaited her.

If you find yourself reading this as you are in a similar place to where Martin was, you are about to be lifted, inspired and awed by the story of a boy and his mum, because as men, when we are in the company of our mum, no matter our age, we always remain deep down, just that, a boy and his mum.

When supporting grieving clients (in my capacity as a Clinical Hypnotherapist and Psychotherapist) who have experienced a sudden loss, and find themselves held hostage to the 'If only I could have'… and 'What if I had…' I have often shared the reference point from author Jamie Anderson:

"Grief, I've learned, is really just love. It's all the love you want to give, but cannot. All that unspent love gathers up in the corners of your eyes, the lump in your throat, and in that hollow part of your chest. Grief is just love with no place to go."

But not everyone who loses a loved one find themselves suffering from grief. When the loss is a long slow gradual affair, where they have the chance to say all the things they want to say and share all the love they have to share, that love finds its way home… every time!

Through his loving heart, honest courage and the compassionate words, Martin tells the story of a son who loved his mum, and in the telling of his story through the pages of *Another Cup of Tea* he will, I am sure, be the light for many to find the strength they need to navigate their own journey in support of their loved ones who find themselves in dementia and on a foggy journey to a distant horizon and a new dawn, on an unknown shore… but who will be taking with them a heart filled with love.

So, do yourself a favour, grab yourself Another Cup of Tea, and enjoy!

Andy McMenemy, Clin.Hyp D.ThHyp (Dist) MHS (Accred)

Preface

How do we cope when dementia robs a parent of their mental capacities and turns them self-destructive or violent? What's the best course of action when even the professional carers are struggling with their interventions?

In this case, the alternative care options were limited as Mum's dementia was quite advanced, so I gave up my job, moved in with Mum through the week and became her full-time carer. This precious time spent with Mum was absolutely priceless. As Mum had always cared selflessly for us (Dad, my brother and myself) I had a very good idea of what caring for Mum could and should look like.

The caring journey was a rollercoaster ride of ups and downs. By journaling the numerous experiences via social media I found a great weight was lifted. I was able to get instant feedback and encouragement from friends and other carers who had been through similar journeys.

The only sure thing in life is that it will end. The one promise I can make to anyone embarking on a care-giving journey is that no matter how challenging it gets in the heat of any given moment, looking back, after the event, you won't regret a single minute. If you have a chance to care for a loved one in their final years, you've been given a rare opportunity indeed.

This book is only a fraction of the journey. Hopefully though it's enough to show that with a brave pill, a good sense of humour and lashings of TLC anyone can learn how to help counter the symptoms of dementia and Alzheimer's disease.

Contents

1. Bootle Lass

There's a scene in the film *The Grinch* where he's hurtling down the mountain, out of control, on the back of an overpowered, motorised sleigh screaming, "Mommy, tell it to stop!" That was me this morning.

One of the symptoms of Mum's dementia is that these personalities keep appearing from nowhere and even as her son of 56 years, I don't recognise any of them! The toughest of the bunch is a girl I call 'Bootle Lass' and it's how I imagine she would have had to be growing up in Bootle, Liverpool in the 1920s and 30s.

I'd offered her a cup of tea this morning, just the way she loves it.

"What do I want with a cup of boiling hot water? I can't drink that!"

Or maybe some cornflakes with her milk warmed up.

"What's this? I don't want bloody cornflakes!"

Then Mum asks, "Why's our bin on the front path?"

"The bin men are coming to collect it," I'd reply.

"Well in all the time I've been here, they've never done that! You're just making it up!"

And so it went on until I mentioned Bootle (I was thinking 'Bootle Lass' but didn't say it of course); the mood lifted, memories came flooding back and off Mum went on a mental journey, back in time to Sidney Road where she lived for the first eight years of her life before they went upmarket and moved to Crosby no less! They moved then to Southport, Tarporley and finally to Chester, all with either her father's work at the time or to escape the bombing of Liverpool during WW2.

Given the feisty energy that 'Bootle Lass' usually brings, I packed us some butties and managed to get Mum into the car for a quick run out to Liverpool.

We headed first to the beach at Crosby where she remembers playing as a child, then down to Bootle for a trip to Sidney Road. Memories flooded back as we pootled around the back streets before heading off down the dock road towards the Liver Buildings, just down from the bank where she used to work at her first job.

Apparently distraction is important with dementia, in this case it worked a treat, well at least until 'Bootle Lass' comes out to play again... gulp!

2. Broken Fire

Normally Mum loves the fire on, regardless of the weather outside. Luckily for me, during my absence the fire broke; in truth it got turned off (thanks Rob) but Mum always thinks we need the gasman to come out if the pilot light is out.

It's the same with the old carriage clock on the mantelpiece; each time it needs winding Mum says, "Your Dad is going to take it to the menders," to which my stock reply is, "Let me see if I can fix it Mum!" She must think I'm such a clever lad as it always gets going again after I've fiddled with it. Funny that!

In spite of the broken fire, Mum dressed for the ongoing heatwave and didn't mention the gasman again; it could be that the fire being on is simply one of those patterns or habits we all fall into. I'm certainly a creature of habit, I see where I get it from now!

I brought Mum breakfast on a tray as usual this morning and now we've just shared a sandwich lunch in the back room, looking into the garden. Radio 3 is on quietly in the kitchen, doors and windows are open getting some draught blowing through and we're settling down this afternoon for a quiet read of our books.

Mum is glued to Ken Pye's books about the history of Liverpool; she's even got a piece of kitchen roll as a bookmark. I find it quite amazing that she knows where she's up to considering she doesn't know I'm even here most of the time. I can walk out of the room and go to the kitchen and she's forgotten I'm here.

The brain is a remarkable thing.

I've asked a couple of times if she fancied a trip out anywhere, hoping for a bit of fresh air, but the energy levels are too low. "My get up and go has got up and gone," she says. So a 'quiet day in' is the recipe for today.

A day to savour methinks.

3. The Calm Before the Storm

As the old sailing proverb goes: Waves rise on silent water.

What appeared to be shaping up to be a calm day, of reading and cups of tea while the rain watered the parched garden, ended up in a violent storm. Mum's usual fretting time can arrive anytime between 3.00pm and 6.00pm; during this time endless amounts of patience and diversions are required to keep the lid from blowing off.

We discussed tea. Who was coming, what we were having and when we'd have it. Five minutes later Mum's got an old outsized coat on, lipstick on and handbag at the ready to go and buy food for the long list of people she's imagined are coming.

Mum's not been to the shops on her own for over six years (as far as we know that is). Instead, we go with her, draw up shopping lists with her, hold her hand or help her with her walker. Today however, Mum was back in 1970-something and we needed food for everyone and that was that.

As things transpired I managed to cook something for tea while Mum fiddled around in her handbag for the list I'd made of what I was cooking and who was coming.

"We need something for tea!" Mum says as she watches me cooking.

"Yes, I'm cooking it now," I reply with a smile.

"What are we having for afters?" she asks.

"Cake?" I suggest.

"Can I see it?" she asks and frowns.

In the end the coat came off and got thrown on the floor, not because she doesn't like my cooking, more because she was getting more and more frustrated that the people she wanted to come couldn't come. (They all passed away many moons ago.)

No amount of diversions can wholly get around someone stamping their feet and demanding a dead relative is here for tea. All I could do was hug her, calm her down, hold her hand, lead her to the table and put a photo on the table with us of her dear father.

Calm was restored to the ship for a short while, but the 'reality' of Mum's belief there was supposed to be a funeral party tonight was rock solid. I've just driven her to the church to see for herself that it wasn't tonight after all.

That's the thing with our 'realities' – to each of us they appear absolutely real and no amount of physical evidence to the contrary can alter that reality. As far as Mum is concerned, her father has just died and all I can do is assure her and go with her reality for a while until it passes again.

4. Driving Miss Daisy

The house must feel like a prison at times, Mum never ventures out alone, only with my brother or myself these days. However, getting out of the house is good for her mental stimulation and today it's a leisurely drive to Buxton for a wander around the shops and the Pavilion Gardens.

I wonder, as Mum gets into the car, if anyone's thought of inventing a car seat for elderly passengers. Mum's shrunk so much in stature now she can hardly see over the dashboard. Maybe I'll bring a cushion next time, it will help to lift her up, hopefully just enough for her to see out of the car window properly.

Mum loves car journeys, she reads out every number plate, poster and road sign, then every shop window and lorry that goes past, like a hyper-observant child who's just learned to read.

As children ourselves (my brother and I) we used to play I Spy on long journeys with Mum and Dad joining in. Now it's like I Spy but without the little book or any clues, just Mum spying anything and everything.

Buxton was busy. There was so much for Mum to take in and explanations were needed for all the new brands and shop signs that didn't make sense to her, like TUI, or Moosh, or Atticus Boo. Her hearing is poor now and her voice is so quiet that in the busy shops it's quite a job to hear her, so we end up going through the motions of saying everything at least three times over.

The dementia brings other challenges though, like balance and coordination. Walking with her, hand in hand, I can feel when she's unsteady and losing her balance, I hold on tight so she feels safe. When getting into or out of the car she can't figure out where the door will open outwards to or where to stand so she's clear of it.

The safety belt provides its own *Generation Game* style challenge, with the straps somehow getting under, over, through handbags, around her walking stick, catching her ear, you name it. She'd laugh her socks off if she could see how something once so 'everyday' had become such a challenge.

We made it back home seconds before the rain came. The safety belt came off easier than it went on. Mum was worn out though and is now resting in the conservatory, listening to the rain on the roof, remembering the similar sound of endless rainy days in the caravan.

5. Midnight Feast

Mum went to bed last night at a relatively early 10pm. I made sure she'd got her hot chocolate and retired to my own room for what I thought would be a well-earned rest.

At 11.45pm I was awoken by the sounds of Mum in the kitchen, light pouring through the back room curtains. Crikey! I thought that was a short night! Then I realised the time. I'd been fast asleep and wrongly thought it was morning.

The sound of Mum pacing up and down is quite familiar now. I can usually tell where she is and what she's up to. In this case though, the array of noises from the kitchen had me wondering.

I listened as her footsteps went from the lounge to the kitchen, from the bedroom to the bathroom, up and down the hall. Flump, flump, flump, the sound of her half-on, half-off slippers as they follow Mum around hanging on for dear life.

Then the kitchen sounds started: the crinkling of plastic wrappers, the slamming of the microwave door (she uses this to warm her drinks up, even when they're already just made). Then the running of the taps, the boiling of the kettle, the opening and closing of the front door, the switching on and off and on of light switches.

The house must have looked like a disco from the outside. I lay there, not wanting to disturb or frighten her, and just listened carefully, vigilant like a night watchman.

Eventually came what I thought were the final set of footsteps up the hall to her bedroom, flump, flump, flump. Then silence.

Sweet silence.

Then more footsteps, flump, flump, flump, Mum heads off up the hall again, light switches off and on, off and on, on and off. Then one last shuffle to her bedroom and a perfect silence was restored. Just the sound of a ticking clock could be heard.

In the morning I got up early to check around and see what kind of a tidying up job was needed. Apart from full cups of tea and hot chocolate in numerous locations, I noticed something out of place in the oven. Four custard cream biscuits had been baked at 230 degrees on a little china saucer to make a new midnight snack – 'Le Custard Crème à la Carbon'.

Next to the microwave was half a cup of hot chocolate, welded to the worktop, and little drips of sticky hot chocolate on all the tops.

By her bed this morning I found two of the drinks she'd prepared and crumbs of some uncooked custard creams… fancy eating them raw, really!

Naturally Mum knows nothing of my discoveries this morning, or her midnight feast last night. She'd either laugh or cry, but knowing Mum, she'd probably laugh.

6. Bloody Mess

As mentioned previously, one of the symptoms of dementia is that Mum is unsteady on her feet even at the best of times. Around the house she uses a stick (when she can find it), otherwise walking from room to room she tends to steady herself on walls and doorframes.

On Wednesday though the inevitable happened, she stumbled backwards, catching her foot on an iron dog that's used to keep the kitchen door wedged open.

Luckily I was with her in the kitchen, she'd stepped backwards, caught her foot, lost her balance and was about to fall through the door into the hallway. Instinctively I reached forward, grabbed her wrists and caught her before she hit the ground. I bent over and pulled her back upright and walked her to the lounge.

No sooner had I got back in the kitchen to make an emergency cup of tea, I heard Mum calling me back saying, "Look what you've done!"

I rushed back in to see blood pouring down Mum's wrists from under her jumper. She pulled up her sleeves and her skin had torn in two places on her fragile wrists, the skin was a good half an inch apart from where it should be and blood was coming from both wounds.

A quick decision was needed, so in the heat of the moment at 5.20pm I covered her wounds loosely with kitchen roll, walked her to the car and drove as quickly as possible to A&E in Macclesfield.

I figured this was the best option as the wounds needed treating ASAP.

We arrived at the hospital at 5.40pm and were met by a 'streaming nurse' who fills out a form, checks the wounds and assesses where to send us. Mum introduces me as her husband Fred and tells the nurse that I'd done this to her.

Not wanting to upset Mum further, I discreetly mouth "d-e-m-e-n-t-i-a" to the nurse who quickly, I hoped, had figured out what was going on but still made notes on the form that wrongly assumed Mum was able to remember where she was, how we'd got there and what had just happened. I mentioned about the choice between calling 999 and driving here and the nurse assures me this was the right decision.

We sat in A&E for over two hours, meanwhile her wounds were healing, which given the skin tears is far from ideal. The call eventually came and a duty doctor came to meet us and examine Mum. I really felt for her, Mum chastised her like a naughty child and gave her both barrels for touching her untreated wrists. Luckily no broken bones, just bruising and the skin tears to stitch up.

Then came a nurse and she was brilliant, ever so gentle. Mum refused painkillers, she just gripped my hands as the skin was pulled back together and she quietly writhed in agony.

Much to my embarrassment Mum kept telling the nurse that I was her husband and I'd done this to her. "Can you see how strong he is?" "Look what he's done!"

The nurse gave me a knowing smile (that Mum couldn't see) and gingerly placed 14 paper stitches over the skin tears, brilliantly pulling back the skin and patiently repairing the open wounds.

We were discharged at about 8.45pm; Mum still hadn't eaten since lunch and wanted chips from town. I couldn't face eating given the situation so said I'd have something when we got home to Poynton.

"What are we going to Poynton for, I don't live there?" Mum asks. "You'll recognise it when we get there Mum," I say hopefully.

We arrived at home and carefully reinstalled Mum in her favourite chair, still clutching a tray of warm chips and asking where Martin was.

I eventually got her to bed, having to help her to bed this time as she couldn't put any pressure on her hands to move. She kept her blood-soaked jumper on underneath her nightdress; the bandage was too big to get the jumper over it without pain.

I managed a couple of hours' sleep that night, waking at 2.00am then 4.00am as Mum got up for the loo. When I got up at 6.45am, Mum was asleep in the lounge, blood had wept through the bandages, so whilst the nurse had given strict instructions for the dressing to stay on for five days, I had to call the district nurse to come and redress it to avoid infection. Naturally, all the dressings were now firmly stuck with blood to her wounds, so to say the nurse did well to re-dress it is an understatement.

The upside to the story is… As Mum rested before the district nurse arrived, I managed to do the unmentionable: I changed the bedding that she won't let me go near and pulled out all the jumpers that she won't let me wash. I laid out clean clothes on her bed and smuggled out the dirty laundry to my car.

I went back into the lounge as though nothing had happened, feeling relieved to have tackled these much-needed chores and Mum looked up at me, all innocent like a child and said, "I'm a bloody mess!" "It's only blood Mum, you've still got plenty left," I said. "It's just as well!" said Mum, followed by the old chestnut, "Just wait until your father gets home!"

7. Body Clocks

A line from an old Phil Collins song runs through my head as I awake in the unexpected dark of 3.45am: "*I can hear through these walls and I hear every sign, every sound.*"

Mum's up, flushing the loo, switching lights on and off, clanking the great doors of the mirrored wardrobes in her bedroom, shuffling barefoot from room to room, possibly on the hunt for her slippers.

Flump, flump, flump, she's found them. Then the sound of her blowing her nose, it runs now and again, uncontrollably like a tap, and takes a good few minutes of best effort but still half-hearted blows for her to complete the task. The loo flushes again.

Flump, flump, flump Mum's off to the kitchen now, she runs the hot water, runs the cold water, fills the kettle, boils the kettle, clanks dishes, fills then empties the bowl in the sink and plays with light switches. If there was some underlying rhythm to this you could set it to music.

I lie there, half-asleep but in vigilant 'Night Watchman' mode, making sure she comes to no harm and sense where she is before I dare to find the arms of Morpheus once more.

Flump, flump, flump she heads for my door. Silence, stillness, I can almost hear her thinking, trying to figure out where she is and what's going on.

She turns, heads to her bedroom, opens and closes a few more drawers, quietly gets dressed, hangs up her dressing gown on the back of the door, makes her bed, then flump, flump, flump back to the kitchen.

A final boil of the kettle suggests this could be the last one before she settles. The lifting of the kettle, the clinking of the spoon in the teacup, the kettle going back down on to its electric base. Flump, flump, flump to the lounge. I hear the lounge door close and picture her sat comfortably in her favourite chair, a cup of tea at the ready and possibly wondering why the clocks say what they do.

A few hours somehow fly by and my alarm goes off. I wonder if I'll be able to get out of bed given the weight of the bags under my eyes. Being an early riser it's a temporary issue, so I quickly get dressed and head off to survey the scene from the wee small hours.

Lights are on in Mum's bedroom, the bathroom and the lounge. The kitchen one is off but there's not as much evidence of shenanigans as I expected. Mum is half-asleep in her favourite chair, listing over to one side, fully dressed and ready for action, her head on a cushion on the arm of the sofa.

"Blimey Mum! You've been up since 3.45am!" I say.

"How do you know that?" she asks, as though I had super powers of intuition.

"I looked at my watch by my bed," I said.

"Well it must be wrong too, like all these clocks in here!"

"Would you like some cereal M' Ladyship?" I ask.

"Oh yes, that would be lovely James!" she replies, playing along with the game we've co-created to get us through these times.

I write this to the reassuring sound of a clock ticking in the back room and in the distance… the sound of a spoon clinking reassuringly on a cereal bowl, and a mother, blissfully unaware of her body clock.

8. Fast a' Worried

The house was quiet at 8.00 this morning. Not a sound from Mum's room, just the church bells in the distance and the occasional 'tap, tap, tapping' of the central heating pipes.

I made myself a pot of fresh coffee, put the radio on, washed up some of the left-over dishes from Mum's late night snacks and pottered around the silent house, noticing odd things in odd places.

Missing from the scene though was a second sugar bowl Mum had left out over the weekend. There's always a full one by the kettle, but for some reason a second one was made using a small striped pottery bowl and sugar from the cupboard.

I've since looked in every cupboard and the striped sugar bowl has literally vanished into not-so-thin air. Maybe it will turn up, maybe it's hiding with the missing hearing aids and numerous other things that disappear during the course of each week.

Mum appeared at her bedroom door at 9.15am, a worried look upon her face and possibly still half-asleep.

"I didn't want to disturb you Mum, you were fast asleep," I said.

"I wasn't fast asleep I was fast a' worried," she replied in all seriousness.

After assuring her everything was OK, I walked her to the lounge where I'd already got a cup of tea waiting for her (made ten minutes earlier in the hope that she'd be up in good time).

"Is it poisoned?" Mum asked with a concerned look.

"Whatever makes you think that Mum?" I ask with a smile.

"Well, I don't know where I am or what's happening!" she replied.

Clearly, the concerns from last night had remained with her and all that endless pacing up and down the hall from her bedroom to the front door, from 10.00pm until midnight, hadn't done anything to help quell the anxiety.

I did wonder as I lay there last night, waiting for the sound of Mum going to bed, if we should get her a Fitbit or something that measures her steps. She must have walked miles last night alone!

Breakfast was served on a tray and the reassuring clink, clink of the spoon on the cereal bowl helped bring the space back to a sense of normality.

At 10.00am Mum notices the clock and declares how late it is and how she'd better get dressed ready for them all coming. Who Mum means by 'them all' remains a mystery at this point.

"Martin, help!" calls Mum from the bathroom. "I've lost all my clothes!"

"They're here on the side of the bath Mum," I reply.

"They're outside on the path!" exclaims Mum with an air of even greater confusion than earlier.

I laugh inwardly and repeat the answer, this time showing her the missing clothes, then head off to let her get dressed in privacy.

"Martin, help!" calls Mum again from the bathroom.

"It's my toenail, it's stuck!" she says in apparent agony.

"Can you walk Mum?" I ask.

"It hurts that much I could bloody fly!" she says.

Her little toe is pointing upwards, it looks as though it may have gone into spasm, so I take her weight off it and walk her gingerly to the lounge where I can have a proper look at the affected toe.

"Ow, ow, ow!" says Mum.

"Ooh, ooh, ooh," she adds, unsure what to do with herself.

"Let me have a look Mum," I say and the problem reveals itself in the light from the front window: a thread from her trousers has caught around her little toenail and is acting like a high tension wire and lifting her little toe up from the others.

I pull out my Swiss Army knife and unlock the scissors.

Mum yells, "Don't cut me, be careful!" as I make a purposeful move towards the offending thread.

"It's OK Mum, my brother's a doctor," I say jokingly…

Snip and it's done, Mum lets out a cry of relief and all is right with the world.

Throughout the morning Mum's been asking where everyone is – her parents, my dad, my brother, Uncle Tom Cobley and all – and even though I may risk speaking too soon, I have managed to assure her and pacify the concerns... thus far at least.

A nice sandwich for lunch, followed by a call to a mobile chiropodist and an appointment made so the risk of further snagging will be countered.

The missing sugar bowl is still nagging me though, so after mowing the lawns this afternoon I'll have another look around, just in case it's balanced, booby-trapped on a shelf edge somewhere, waiting to fall out on someone!

9. Back to the Kitchen

I arrived this Monday morning to find Mum half on and half off the sofa. To say she looked drained would be an understatement. She was fully dressed and from what I could tell by the rest of the house, hadn't been to bed on Sunday night, just locked up, closed the curtains and fallen asleep where she was.

Mum didn't want any breakfast, just another cup of tea. In times like these where Mum's on low energy start to the day, I let her rest to regain her strength and get on with a few jobs around the house, making sure not to make any noise. Whenever I do head to the kitchen it's always met with a weak sounding "Hello?" from Mum in the lounge.

There have been so many carers coming and going over the past few years, it must be so very confusing for her.

I made us a sandwich for lunch and Mum was coming round by this point, able to sit further up the chair at least and making approving "Yum, yum!" noises as she tucked into what could be her first meal since Sunday evening.

After lunch, a couple of hours go by before Mum comes to the back of the house, where I'm busy pottering, to ask if I'd like some lunch.

"No thanks Mum, we've just had some!" I reply.

"Yes, but I thought you may still be hungry!" Mum replies hoping for a taker.

Back to the kitchen goes Mum, and then returns within the minute.

"Would you like some lunch?"

"No thanks Mum, we've just had some!" Back to the kitchen. Silence.

Two minutes later Mum returns, this time holding a mini pizza from the fridge.

"Would you like some of this for your lunch?"

"No thanks Mum, we've just had some!" Back to the kitchen. Silence.

Two minutes later Mum returns.

"Have you seen your brother?"

"He's at work Mum," I say.

"I've not seen him for ten days," says Mum.

I know he was here over the weekend, however I've learned not to correct her about anything, it only confuses things, and so I attempt to change the subject. Back to the kitchen. Silence.

Three minutes pass by before Mum returns holding her cup of tea.

"If he comes back, will you give your brother this cup of tea?"

"Will do Mum," I say, wondering if this will be the last offer before she assumes the welcoming familiarity of the comfy chair.

Nope. Back to the kitchen!

Then the sound of her nails drumming on the worktops.

This usually indicates thinking. Silence.

A whole ten minutes pass by, I then hear all kinds of noises in the kitchen, so guess there's something on its way.

More sounds of nails drumming on the worktops.

I hear Mum's footsteps again.

"Would you like some lunch?"

"No thanks Mum, we've just had some! Are you hungry?" I ask noticing she'd only eaten half her sandwiches.

"Oh no, I'm not hungry," exclaims Mum rubbing her tummy as though she's eaten for England today.

Back to the kitchen! I hear the kettle boil, the fridge door open and close. The crinkling sounds of a packet of something being opened. The bread bin opening and closing.

Then silence.

Footsteps down the hall again.

Mum heads to the conservatory and says, "Oh, it's not there!"

"What's that Mum?" I ask.

"A tin of syrup," she replies.

"Do you want me to find it Mum?"

"What?" she replies.

"A tin of syrup," I say.

"A what?"

"A tin of syrup."

"Who for?"

"You Mum, you just asked for a tin of syrup!" I say struggling to find the right volume to be heard without disturbing the neighbours.

"Oh no, I'm fine," she says.

To be sure, I escort Mum to the kitchen anyway. Two rounds of bread are buttered and waiting on the breadboard. A cup of tea waits beside them.

So she was hungry after all.

I reach into the cupboard directly below where the breadboard is and pull out the tin of syrup.

"What's that?" Mum asks.

"A tin of syrup just like you wanted Mum," I say.

"Oh and there it was all the time!" declares Mum.

Mum completes making her second helping of lunch and shuffles to the lounge, hopefully ready to make up for the gap left by only eating half her lunch earlier.

I head to the back room and have no sooner sat down before the sound of shuffling feet can be heard heading to the back again.

"Would you like a syrup sandwich?"

"No thanks Mum, we've just had some lunch!"

This time I head to the kitchen as Mum goes back to the lounge. I tidy up the crumbs and search for the syrup tin, just to see if it went back to the normal place. It's not there. After a quick look in all the cupboards, the missing tin eventually reveals its shiny green, white and gold branding on the middle shelf of the fridge.

The latest search through all the cupboards reminds me… there's still no sign of the mystery sugar bowl!

10. Dark Side of the Mum

Bedtime last night went without a hitch, Mum retired to bed with her hot chocolate drink and no fuss whatsoever. I stayed awake until about 11.30pm just to listen out for her in case she got up again for some nocturnal hall pacing, fortunately all was quiet.

The rain on the conservatory roof woke me up early, but as the house was still quiet I managed to drift back off into a dream. At 5.30am though Mum was up and about, the rain must have woken her too and she headed for the kitchen to start her day in the dark.

I could hear her making her own cereal, her own cup of tea and the reassuring clinking of the spoon on the cereal bowl as she settled down in the lounge for her early breakfast. On most 'normal days' Mum doesn't want breakfast until after 9.00am at least, so this was clearly not an ordinary start to her day.

When I went to check on her at 7.30am Mum was fretting over Dad and how come he'd died and nobody had told her? She wanted to know the full story. Her line of questioning was that intense I was half expecting her to ask me for my name, rank and number!

The questions though were about the how, when, where, and whilst I have successfully diverted her away from this topic over recent weeks, her stress levels were high as she clearly couldn't make sense of anything.

As compassionately as possible I went over the circumstances of Dad's departure and showed her the note she'd written at the time, which is propped up on a stand with his ashes on the sideboard. I kept answers to questions as short as possible and tried to change the subject at every opportunity. It was quite futile.

Suddenly a dark cloud appeared to float over her. I was now the enemy, I wasn't her son, that was the other Martin, it was my fault she was here in this house and there was no consoling her, not from tears as you may expect, but from the darkness of her latest thoughts.

"You're taking over from the nurses now are you?" said Mum as I went to the secure box to get her tablets.

"I would Mum but they won't let me wear a nurse's dress," I say hoping to lighten the tension.

"Well you couldn't look any dafter if you bloody well tried anyway!" she said keeping her best frown going.

I left Mum to drink her tea and collect her thoughts. She was soon up and about and paced the hall, checked all the rooms, looking everywhere for 'the others'.

Lunchtime eventually came around, Mum turned up at the kitchen door wearing her three sizes too big coat, and in her hand was a pair of scissors. I wondered about what was next on her agenda. I dared to ask and got a mouthful, apparently she was going to the garden to cut off some plants she didn't like, but only if it met with my approval. Sir!

I told her I loved her and asked if she'd like anything for lunch which was sternly met with a "Don't try and change the subject!" and a threatening wave of the scissors.

By this time Mum had got as far as the kitchen worktop and was looking out of the window at the dustbins left out by "some idiot who should know better". That'll be me by the way. The bin men come every Tuesday.

On the worktop was a sharp kitchen knife, I reached across and managed to remove this from sight just in case two weapons looked even more appealing to her than just the scissors alone. Luckily this went unseen and I carried on attempting to prepare a lunch for two people who doubtless both had butterflies and stomachs in knots.

I assure Mum as best I can that everything's OK and she's safe here, even though she kept suggesting she wanted to go home and never come back here. I managed to persuade Mum to take a seat back in the lounge, knowing the furnace-like heat would be enough to make her take the coat off.

The plan worked, the coat came off and another cup of tea with a chocolate digestive would help to provide some normality to the proceedings. I aimed to help her to settle by sitting with her and holding her hand. It worked.

Lunch was rejected and instead replaced by the chocolate digestives; this was mainly down to not knowing what she fancied and not being hungry really.

The district nurse was due today to change the dressing on her wounds. She duly arrived and changed the dressing without any fuss. Mum had by this time completely forgotten the earlier stress and anxiety she felt and was busy enjoying her book about Liverpool history by Ken Pye.

I hid the scissors and did a few chores to reclaim that 'calm space within' that has to exist in order for days like these to wash over me. I learned many years ago that humility could have the effect of dissipating anger. I'm glad I'd already had that lesson as it proved invaluable today!

Anyway, there's a knock-on effect of Mum not eating a proper lunch, even if it is usually only half of one… the fretting about tonight's tea has started and now the contents of the freezer are coming out… got to dash!

11. Autumn Leaves

"What are you doing Mum?" I ask as Mum heads out to the garden with a wicker wastepaper basket.

"Somebody has kindly dropped leaves everywhere!" declares Mum, somewhat taken aback by the audacity of the situation.

Mum proceeds to pick up each and every fallen leaf off the lawn, luckily not too many just yet, but enough to fill the basket until it's brimming with red, gold and brown leaves. She brings them back into the house, still astounded why someone would even think of dropping them all on this garden of all gardens.

Luckily, the council provide us with a bin for garden waste, so after searching around for a suitable place to put the leaves, I suggest the 'green bin' as a good place for them. Mum obliges, 'tutting' all the while at the things some people do. I go along with the story and tut too, looking skywards to emphasise the point.

Earlier in the day I'd been on the hunt for Mum's stock of tablets, these are normally kept high up, out of reach on top of the kitchen cupboards. The tablets come in blister packs, folded like lightweight books, a book for each week, a blister for each day and a lot of blanks where other tablets would go if needed.

Mum used to take 12 tablets a day (now only two); it became a daily drama when Dad was still with us – which tablets had been taken, whose tablets belonged to whom, which tablets to take when and have today's been taken or are these tomorrow's?

When Dad died we found boxes and boxes of medications in his wardrobes, in drawers and in boxes. I ended up filling bin-bags with them and keeping them in the shed, ready to go back to the pharmacy in manageable amounts.

Anyway, the blister packs come in an open-ended card box, four blister packs for the month, each neatly marked up to make it easy to see where we're up to. The normal routine is to keep one blister pack in a locked metal safe box in the lounge. We dispense Mum's tablets from here each day and top up her supply from the box on top of the kitchen cupboard. Theoretically.

I hunted around, this time with a sense of urgency as nothing would surprise me these days and I quickly checked and double-checked all the potential hiding places for the missing full pack containing four blister packs!

Bedroom, bathroom, kitchen, lounge, conservatory, drawers, wardrobes, cupboards, the 'strand' behind Mum's chair corner, each empty space providing impetus to check the next potential hiding place.

As often is the case when something goes missing, it's always the last cupboard we open that reveals the missing item. In this case there were a few bonuses. Set right to the back of a kitchen cupboard, the one Mum sometimes confuses as the fridge, I see the white of the blister pack reflecting my torchlight.

Relief is quickly dispelled by the pong of something that should have been in the fridge. A pack of strawberries sat neatly alongside a pack of cooked chicken slices and a pack of sliced cheese. As you'd expect, no missing sugar bowl, I'd already checked here on previous weeks, but at least the tablets have been safely found and put away!

Later that evening I thought I'd treat myself and attempt to watch the football. Mum was pretty much like a limpet much of the day and the evening proved no exception.

She asked if I'd like a cup of tea 18 times during the first half, on the 18th request I said yes as she was clearly frustrated at my preference to go at least half an hour without a drink.

Mum returned with a tray. On the tray was a cup, a teapot filled with hot water, an empty milk jug and a sugar bowl. These teapot routines are just like the scenes where a child makes a pretend cup of tea with those little red plastic tea sets in the back garden, where the child pretends to pour the tea and the parent pretends to sip it and say, "Ooooh thank you, what a lovely cup of tea!" and the child smiles at the parent's stupidity.

In our case, Mum is so sharp I expect that such pretence would be met with a "Don't be daft, there's no tea in that cup!" or words to that effect. So, I break from the football to find a teabag and milk and drink the unwanted tea just for the break it may provide.

Manchester City go on to win the game. Mum's happy doing her colouring so I watch the United game too. On the football front, Mum and Dad used to have friends who were involved with the City supporters club, so they were always around 'the beautiful game'. Mum also used to date a Liverpool player before she met Dad and subsequently, if ever she sees a football game she thinks it's Liverpool playing and duly shouts, "Come on Liverpool!"

The Manchester United game got its fair share of interruptions too. Only seven offers of tea but things got serious when it came to supper. I daren't leave Mum to make her own supper as she "doesn't know where anything is in this house".

Lemon cheese butties are what she decides upon. I set out all the components and potter around while she makes the sandwiches, slowly making her a cup of hot chocolate and giving her the space to do the sandwich-making herself without her feeling incapable, a risk we all face if we do too much for a loved one I guess.

I'm feeling quite tired by this time, so suggest it's bedtime. Mum miraculously agrees and takes her butties and hot chocolate to bed.

I don't hear another peep out of Mum until 7.00am.

Fingers crossed she doesn't see the lawn… it's covered in leaves again!

12. Mind the Gap!

Somebody must be watching over us.

Crunch, crackle, crackle. I hear something like the sound of a tree branch being broken. The sound crackles out at the precise moment Mum's foot had wedged between the pavement, the road and the side of the car.

"What was that?" I exclaim, clearly concerned about its source.

"What was what?" says Mum, apparently unable to hear (or feel) what I'd heard.

I'd parked the car as close to the kerb as possible to avoid such a calamity. We'd been into the chemist only to find they'd run out of what we'd gone for and just been through the delicate rigmarole of getting Mum out of the car.

Getting back into the car again, she'd somehow inserted her foot down into the gap between the car and the kerb and then twisted herself to get into the car seat. Yikes, I hope that's not a leg break I think to myself and carefully and gingerly guide her leg out of the gap to a chorus of 'Oohs' and 'Aahs'.

Once the leg is back in its rightful place, in front of Mum as she sits back into the car seat, I double check her leg.

"Can you put any weight on it Mum?" I ask.

"Weight on what?" says Mum, continuing the game of 'hey, pardon, what' we'd been playing all day.

"Your leg Mum, is it OK?"

"Oh yes, that's fine!" she says, confused at why I'd even be asking such a silly question.

We drive back down the delightful and picturesque A6 in Stockport. All the way, waves of that feeling where you feel someone else's pain flood through me as I imagine Mum actually breaking her leg. It's funny as I'm not at all squeamish when it comes to blood and wounds, it's just the thought of someone else's pain that goes right through me.

We arrive back home and I monitor the first steps as I uninstall her from the front seat of the car. There's no walking stick today so only two arms, a handbag and a fleece jacket to contend with while attempting the technically challenging 'uncoupling of the seatbelt' manoeuvre.

Mum walks to the house holding my hand for guidance and no pain is visible as she steps up into the house and walks unaided to the lounge.

As she steps into the house she calls out, "Hellooo, hellooo!?" to whoever may have been here in the old days.

"Looks like there's nobody in Mum!" I say as I follow her in.

"I know!" says Mum as though she'd known this all along.

It's moments like these when I secretly wonder if Mum is actually fully 'compos mentis' cunningly recruited by the Russians and this is all part of an elaborate plot!

Na Zdorovie!

13. Detachment

It's amazing just how much stuff we hold on to in life, believing that someday it may come in handy for something.

I had the bright idea to sort through some boxes of 'mixed stuff' today, with Mum supervising what she wanted and what she didn't. Had Mum been her old self, minus the vascular dementia, then I'm sure that 99% of the stuff we found today would have gone back into a box or a drawer for that day when it's 'just what we were looking for'.

It's a different story now though. With the dementia comes a detachment from stuff, in fact much of it only serves to confuse Mum further, so subsequently I've been putting stuff out of her sight into boxes, drawers and cupboards. Given the frequency of my stays here, we were getting a bit short of some free cupboard space so out came these aforementioned boxes to be sorted through.

Much of this stuff would actually be useful to someone so it's more a question of condensing the space it takes up by reducing some of the packaging, spare bags, sleeves and old ice cream tubs.

Mum was surprisingly detached from all the stuff I kept pulling out of boxes, like rabbits out of a magician's hat. "Do you want this Mum?" I'd ask. "That's not mine, that must belong to the lady who lives here!" Mum would state, matter-of-factly.

In truth, the lady who used to live here died over 20 years ago, so I put everything like this to one side and attempt to find something Mum actually recognises.

"How about this Mum?" I'd say, lifting up a bag of trimmings. "Oh, I don't recognise any of that!" says Mum, happy to see it disappear.

And so went the afternoon.

In between all this, I've noticed that Mum hallucinates quite frequently, seeing things that only she can see, but always asking me to affirm what she's seeing. I naturally don't want to make her think she's imagining things all the time, so I often just say, "Oh, sorry, I missed that!" which is generally a satisfactory response it seems.

Today's hallucinations were auditory as well and Mum kept asking, "Did you hear that?" "What Mum?" I'd ask. "Somebody shouted!" Mum says. "Oh, sorry, I missed that!" I'd reply.

Nine times out of ten when Mum hears something she heads to the front door to investigate. Nine times out of ten there's nothing there, but at least Mum is getting plenty of steps in! What with the imaginary voices and the missing people she's constantly looking for, she must be doing about 4,000 steps a day!

On the food front, last week's fruit salad was such a success, somehow Mum remembered and asked if we could have it again this week. I got all the ingredients out, plus a bowl, a chopping board and a relatively blunt knife for safety.

I let Mum make the whole thing, with me merely watching over from a safe distance. The thought struck me as Mum chopped away at the apples just how many meals she must have made over the years. If we take off say two weeks a year for holidays, this still means she's made about 21,000 meals over the course of her marriage from 1952 to 2013 when the towel got thrown in and Dad took over.

The fruit salad took quite some time, but it was of course time well spent in the form of a useful distraction. Mum kept saying how blunt the bloody knife was and then realising it was the wrong way up and turning it round to see that it did work after all.

Even with the distractions, Mum still asked about who else was coming for tea. I lost count as we sailed way past the 20 times mark. The same question kept on coming up throughout tea and then again as we ate the fruit salad.

The stock answer I give nowadays, aside from "I don't know" is "we've got plenty in if anyone comes!" and this is working, apart from the attachment Mum still has for what we've actually got in the fridge and the cupboards. Luckily the butler (me) is good at guided tours of the kitchen so these tend to pacify M' Ladyship's 'need to know'.

Talking of the butler… he carried out his new Monday morning cupboard checking routine and found a now furry platter of salmon sandwiches, soft crisps and shrivelled tomatoes. They'd possibly been there since Friday. They had at least been placed in the cupboard M' Ladyship often mistakes as being the fridge.

Perhaps some suitably printed labels for the cupboards may be in order?

Who knows?

14. Degrees of Difficulty

"What's this?" asks Mum, pointing to a form I'd just filled in for her at the chemist's in sunny Stockport.

"It's the form they needed filling in Mum," I reply.

"I can see that but why does it say 'son' here?" she asks and I can sense what's coming.

"That's because I'm your son Mum," I say, hoping that will do the job.

"How can you be my son when you're my husband?" Mum asks and I notice, out of the corner of my eye, all the women in the shop suddenly stop their conversations and start looking our way. Like one of those old Westerns where the stranger walks into a crowded bar and it all goes deadly quiet!

Tumbleweed blows down the dusty street outside. I reach for my wallet like a gunslinger and produce my ID in the blink of an eye, deep down knowing full well it's not going to make even the slightest bit of difference. Mum reads the ID card…

"Martin Owen Dewhurst, yes, that's you, my husband!" she states with an absolute degree of certainty.

Luckily, we were saved by the chemist who came out to check the form and ask a few of her own questions.

All done and dusted, I manage to get Mum reinstalled in the car without any potential broken limbs and hope the other customers in the shop manage to put together enough evidence to conclude what was actually going on.

The fairly long journey home was at least full of signs to read and planes to watch in the sky. As we arrived home though the struggle took us in a new direction.

"Where's this?" Mum asks as I get her to the door without her falling (she was very unsteady on her feet today).

"It's your house Mum," I reply, confidently.

"My house? Get away with your bother my house!" Mum replied and flung her handbag angrily into the hallway in disgust.

She stands outside, looking like she's about to refuse to enter and leaving me, for one of those moments where time stands still, wondering what will happen next.

"Home again, home again!" I say knowing Mum likes to finish off any verse you care to start.

"It may be your bloody home, but it's never mine, I've never seen this place before!!" she says without even a 'jiggety-jig' just getting herself in quite a tizz.

I somehow get Mum to step into the hall and show her into the lounge, reassuring her that all her favourite things are here and there and there and there.

"Yes, I know all that, but this isn't my house and you bloody well know it!" she scolds.

"How about a nice cup of tea Mum?" I ask, hoping to ease the tension.

"Yes please, don't put anything in it though!" she says.

I calm the butterflies by doing some serious sink cleaning. Bleach and boiling water work a treat and once it's sparkling again I head to the lounge with another cup of tea.

"Have you put any poison in it?" Mum asks in all seriousness.

"No Mum, we're completely out of stock, I used a teabag instead," I joke, like we're acting out our roles in some 1970s sitcom or something.

Mum says nothing, just mutters a polite thank you for the tea but you can tell she's still adamant this isn't her house and there's nothing anyone could say to alter that view.

I head to the back room to start prepping for some DIY. Mum follows me five minutes later and asks where the daughter of the house has gone. I tell her I haven't seen anyone.

The idea of a 'degrees of difficulty scale' (DOD) enters my head, like a clap-o-meter only for measuring butterflies in tummies.

Whilst most of today went fairly smoothly, I'm going to give the day based on this afternoon's performance a nine on the 'DOD' scale.

I wonder if nurses have a similar scale for dealing with challenging behaviours?

Ah well, only seven more hours to go to bedtime!

15. Party Night

I could sense there was something afoot last night as Mum was trying to get me to distract the carer. I had a few of my own tasks to do, so listened from the safety of the back room as the carer did her level best to sit for 30 minutes with Mum and make small talk.

Once she'd gone, almost sprinting out of the door, I made sure Mum was refreshed with another cup of tea and a nice book to read. I headed back to the back room and had no sooner sat down than I heard the unexpected sound of clinking, rattling, shuffling and rustling.

Mum was on a mission, so I listened intently to the activities knowing full well I'd have a bit of tidying up to do. I went back to Mum about 15 minutes later, just to make sure there were no flames involved or sharp objects and Mum asked, "What time are they supposed to be coming?"

"Who's that Mum?" I asked, quite surprised at the latest idea.

"All of them, I thought it was Party Night?" she replied, surprised herself that I hadn't heard.

"I'll keep my ears open in case anyone calls Mum," I say, going along with the game.

"Rightio!" says Mum, keen for me to get out of the way.

I head to the back room and tune in from a distance once more. It's like a radio play without words where you have to create your own mental pictures of what's actually going on in another room.

The rustling of plastic bags was soon followed by the crinkling of what sounded like a multipack of crisps. Then the sound of cutlery, lots of cutlery. Lots of steps in and out of the kitchen, back and forth from the lounge. I could hear the drawers being opened and closed on the old sideboard, the obvious sounds of someone looking for long-lost essential things.

Then silence. Sweet silence.

I leave it for another 15 minutes just to make sure it's a proper silence, not just a temporary lull in the proceedings. I head back to the lounge to see Mum fast asleep in her chair, a lukewarm cuppa cradled lovingly in her hands.

On the dining table is the result of her busyness. In the kitchen, no mess as such, just the usual tops to wipe down, unusual things hidden in cupboards and things to put away, but not half as much as it sounded like.

I bring Mum a replacement cuppa, she's recharged her batteries again with that quick nap and is ready to dive into her Liverpool history book again.

I did toy with the idea of suggesting earlier that nobody was coming, then instantly rejected the idea, as I knew it would have upset Mum to have gone to all that trouble for nobody to be coming.

As it transpired, 'Party Night' didn't get mentioned again and by bedtime she was worn out, ready for bed and glad of a hand to hold and someone to guide her safely to her room.

Needless to say, I got up early and made sure everything was restored to its normal place. No children were harmed in the making of this party and Mum's none the wiser this morning about what went on the night before.

As it is every night and every day for that matter, I treasure each moment like it could be our last.

The bottom line is… Mum's teaching me to be a loving son.

Anyone got a hanky?

16. Bootle Book

I arrived this Monday morning to the usual array of misplaced items. Cream cheese in the baking cupboard, all the fruit in a different bowl, biscuits on plates in a few random places, books missing from where I left them and nearly all the cutlery there is in the house out on the table.

As well as the newly acquired skills of subject changing, I've also had to learn to be a dab hand at putting things away discreetly, so Mum doesn't see the process and therefore doesn't worry.

The table had been set for even more people than Thursday night last week. This time we had birthday napkins out for each place, which did make me wonder about whether or not I should ask whose birthday it was. I opted for the safer option of not mentioning it and while Mum went to the loo, everything disappeared off the table into the kitchen and into drawers.

We did some more digging today, pulling out numerous boxes, bags and files of old stuff from old places. One of the treasures was an old book of Bootle, postcards and photos from the good old days when Mum used to live there.

I've noticed that Mum's memory flows in and out like the tide. Fingers crossed, if I can catch Mum when the tide is in, memory-wise, there are loads of old photos that need names adding to faces. It's one of those things that only Mum will know now and she does still have lucid moments where the past becomes clear again.

I've got a touch of the 'dreaded lurgy' at the moment so I am keeping my distance, obviously not wanting Mum to get anything. The Gods were with us today as I was able to keep a safe distance yet keep Mum entertained with newly discovered albums and the Bootle book, which has been read many times over already.

Missing persons wise, Mum's mostly been asking for my brother and her Mum, almost from the minute I got there. Breakfast, lunch and dinner all came and went without a hitch. I also somehow managed to convince Mum that there was no church function to go to tonight and if anything she was relieved at not having to rush.

"We'll have to get another copy of this Bootle book for Taid," said Mum, not realising it was his copy of the book that she'd acquired when Taid, her Dad, died in 1984.

"Yes we will!" I say, and it's enough it seems to keep Mum happy at the moment.

Mum's not slept at all today, so hopefully I'll be able to bring her a hot chocolate at 10.00pm and get a relatively early night myself! At least that was the thought around 8.00pm!

At 10.00pm I reported to M' Ladyship with her hot chocolate. She suggested she was ready for bed and I brought said hot chocolate to her bedside table and put her night light on.

Mum is getting good at pretending to go to bed, then staying up to do various tasks that all could have been done much earlier.

By midnight, Mum was still almost-nearly-just-about getting into bed, prior to this the front door had been opened and closed three times, the kettle had boiled twice and the microwave had been on twice too. The loo had been flushed, the lounge lights turned on and then off, then on and off once more for good measure. The same happened with the kitchen lights.

At 6.00am I was awoken by M' Ladyship.

"Is there anybody in there?" Mum asks tentatively into the darkness.

"Yes, it's only me Mum," I reply, still hoping for another hour of sleep.

"Oh, I didn't know you were in here!" Mum says, sounding pleasantly surprised she's not alone.

"Can I get you anything?" Mum asks, oblivious to the actual time.

"Just another forty winks please," I beg.

"Oh, all right, I'll just close this door," Mum whispers and flumps off down the hall.

Then I hear the front door open, sounding like a giant oak door that creaks slowly open on any good Hammer Horror film and someone says, "You rang Sir?"

My first thought is WD40.

The door opens and closes two more times after this. I suspect she's hoping the milkman has been.

It's still dark, so next I hear the light routine, click, click, click… Click, click, click, there's almost a rhythm to it. Next goes the kettle, then the chinking of china cups on the glass chopping board, then a teaspoon being dropped on the worktop.

"Aaaaaand cue the curtains," and yes, the curtains get drawn to greet the somehow unexpected darkness of a November morning.

Footsteps are flumping to the lounge. Footsteps flumping to the kitchen. Footsteps flumping to the lounge. Footsteps flumping up the hall again to a standstill right outside my door. Footsteps flumping back to the kitchen. The re-boiling of the kettle.

It all goes quiet, like the guns falling silent on armistice (I imagine the very silence, having watched numerous WW1 films over recent days).

Mum doesn't hear the declared truce though and heads back into the no man's land of the kitchen, the kettle boils, the microwave door slams and pings at one minute. The clunk of the microwave door being opened. Footsteps flumping to the lounge...

Silence again. I check the time. It's 6.50am. More footsteps are flumping and another kettle is filling and boiling.

I lie there like a character from *Tom and Jerry*, imagining matchsticks straining to keep my sleep-heavy eyelids open. I dig deep to get beyond the sore throat and fizzy sensation at the back of my nose and pretend this is my first day as M' Ladyship's butler. Dressed, washed and bed made, I go in to check Mum's OK.

As I suspected, she's surrounded by three full cups of tea... well, one looked like hot milk and two were still quite hot black tea. She's sat in her favourite chair and watching the sun come up and lighting up the clouds.

"Did you sleep well?" Mum asks.

"Wonderful thanks Mum, did you?" I fib diplomatically.

"Like a log!" says Mum.

Och well, there's always tonight!

17. The Service

"What time's the service tonight?" Mum asks in a replay of an old concern.

"Ooh, the church is closed tonight, it's Wednesday!" I reply, hoping it will suffice.

"Nobody's been to discuss the arrangements!" says Mum, ignoring any alternative I propose.

And so the day progressed, from worry to worry, from unanswerable question to unacceptable response, interspersed with requests for telephone numbers for long dead relatives. The challenge for any carer, I see this as there's one here as I write, is distracting someone who's so engrossed in a subject nothing will do to divert their attention.

"Your Dad's not got out of bed to sort anything out either," says Mum, right outside the bedroom where he used to sleep.

"Is he still in there now?" I ask, wondering if he will manifest for a while and lend a hand.

"He most certainly is!" says Mum, pushing past me to give him what for.

"Oh, he must have gone without saying anything!" says Mum, as she sees the empty bed.

"Another cup of tea Mum?" I ask, in an attempt to move us along from this stickiness.

"Oh, yes please!" says Mum, almost as though this was her first of the day rather than the umpteenth.

I make Mum some lunch while I'm at it, I'm not too hungry myself as the 'dreaded lurgy' has taken hold now and my throat hurts to swallow anything. All day I've been saying, "I'm keeping my distance Mum, I have a sore throat and you wouldn't like it," and all day Mum's been sympathising one second then standing even closer than normal the next.

Mum and I dabble a bit on the family tree, we flick through the old photo albums again, we find a few books that often help to distract Mum from the worries when they arrive, but nothing really works today.

The theme is constant: 'the service', who is coming, when are we going, who's coming back for food afterwards. These thoughts unite and lead Mum consistently to the thought that she needs to do the shopping, even though it was all done and put away this morning and the cupboards are all full.

"Salmon for dinner tonight Mum," I suggest.

"How many for?" Mum asks hopefully once more.

"Just you and me Mum," I reply like I'm about to wear out that phrase.

"Just you and me? What about the rest of them?" Mum asks, literally astounded.

"They'll be hungry after the service!" says Mum still convinced it's really happening tonight.

"I'll do plenty just in case Mum," I suggest, knowing this also works to dispel the worry.

A silent pause in proceedings, just like the ones you get on Radio 3 between the music... then...

"Don't die will you Martin, I don't know what I'd do," Mum says.

"I'll do my best not to for a while Mum," I say, wondering if I'll actually see the week out.

Mum's been training for her 'Standing in the Way' Gold Medal today. Her best moves have been in four different doorways. She stands, tries to retrieve a thought she's just had from somewhere and we're literally stuck, frozen in time like two statues unable to move. The judges gave her straight nines for her work in the kitchen earlier; whatever it is that needs doing in the kitchen, Mum knows exactly where to go to stop the job in its tracks.

Aside from the coping humour of the situations we get into as a mother and son getting back together for a farewell reunion concert after 36 years, the darker realities of Mum's immediate concerns are far from easy to shift.

I ask about who the service is for, thinking it's just one person, but the reality is Mum doesn't know herself. It's Muriel, her sister, mostly today, I show her the photo of her and Muriel in the garden in Crosby, she laughs out loud, then returns to the potential list of people being buried – her Dad, then me, then my brother, each answer coming out then wanting to go back in again as though on a 'didn't mean to say that' piece of elastic.

It was another 6.30am start this morning, I've done these early starts most of my working life and enjoyed them all, however to achieve this consistently I'd make sure I was in bed for 10.00pm the night before at the latest. These days that's a distant luxury and the present circumstances mean my candle is well and truly burnt at both ends!

Mum's just come in wearing a suitably funeral-like coat to ask for my approval.

"It's lovely Mum, it really suits you, let's have dinner first" I say, like a politician.

Mum agrees and for now the pressure is off for a wee while.

Anyway, here's to a quiet evening ahead and minimal shenanigans!

18. Saving it Up

The day started quietly and stayed like this. Well almost.

Mum had slept in the lounge and complained of 'feeling awful' as I went to check on her this morning. I'm fairly sure this must be the shock of thinking you're decades younger than you are, then waking up in a 91-year-old body.

I'd left Mum nicely tucked in last night at 11.00pm. The fire on low, a cosy warm blanket over her legs and a single lamp on, a cup of hot chocolate by her side. It was so quiet through the night I kept waking up to listen, such is the routine of disturbed nights currently. I did wonder if she'd still be with us in the morning it was that quiet.

As the sun rose, I brought Mum her first brew, soon to be followed by her breakfast, then numerous other brews, biscuits and each time the response was the same...

"I've got no energy left," she'd say.

"Are you happy sitting here Mum?" I'd ask, just to be sure.

"I'm fine, I just need to rest," she'd reply, still keen on finding the missing energy reserves.

By lunchtime Mum was still content to sit/lie where she was but did make a special effort to sit up for the beans on toast.

The afternoon continued much in the same way, Mum having naps between fresh cups of tea left to go cold until the Poynton clock struck four. Mum shuffled her way to the loo, the slowest shuffle you could imagine really, her energy all but gone, or so it appeared.

"Well, I suppose I'd better get myself decent!" said Mum as she stood in the hallway

"That sounds good Mum," I say to gee her along.

Mum heads slowly for the bathroom, then the bedroom. Not soon after she calls out for help in finding her clothes. I open drawers and wardrobes so everything's to hand, then leave her to complete the task.

A good 45 minutes later and Mum emerges from the bedroom asking about dinner, who's coming, what we'll have, where we'll eat etc.

"Salmon tonight Mum," I say, excited myself at the thought of it.

"Ooh, yum, yum," says Mum and we head off slowly down the hall to make another cup of tea to keep her going until it's time to start the cooking.

The carer is due tonight and we don't know what time she'll be coming so I somehow manage, between the barrages of unanswerable questions, to put off the cooking until 5.00pm.

I get all the ingredients out – new potatoes, rocket salad, baby tomatoes and salmon steak – then Mum starts to put them all back into the fridge. I manage to thwart this by suggesting we have some cutlery for the table and then make a start with the cooking before Mum comes back to stand in the way. Mum watches intently as I prepare and cook the meal, all the while increasing her lines of questioning to include the possible funeral entourage who may also want to be fed.

The questioning continues at pace during the eating of the meal, meanwhile I've got Mum's salmon steak in the corner of my eye, wondering if tonight she'll be wanting to leave half her meal and pass the fish over to me. Amazingly she doesn't and proceeds to eat everything, just leaving the skin!

I make Mum her post meal brew and head off to the back to call home and write this. My break lasts a good ten minutes before Mum's back, this time to finalise arrangements for the funeral.

Yes, the funeral has come back to haunt Mum again. I check with her to see who it may be this time and she goes through a few options before deciding on Muriel again to be the subject of tonight's thoughts.

The shenanigans went on until the Poynton church bells struck seven. Prior to which Mum had got her funeral coat on, lipstick, walking stick and handbag, she was ready for walking up to the church.

I tried a whole arsenal of diversions, none of which got anywhere near the target and merely led to Mum standing by the front door ready to walk to church. The moment was like one of those TV adverts where a child is about to run off to another country and the parent is waiting to see how far they'll actually go.

One last-ditched attempt at convincing Mum that the funeral wasn't tonight involved mentioning about all the funerals she'd been to and had there ever been an evening one? That and the fact it was getting pretty chilly stood by the open door, the drizzle falling on the roof of the carport added weight to my argument and the seed of doubt I'd sown in her mind about the actual dates and Mum backed down.

She'd gone from simmering anger and annoyance with me for not telling her about the funeral tonight to 'give-us-a-hug' in the blink of an eye and nobody knew, just Mum's imaginary entourage and myself. It's not that I wanted anything by way of recognition here, it's just that a standing ovation wouldn't have gone amiss.

We'll never know what did the trick there, the main thing is Mum is now sat comfortably once more in the lounge. Her coat is off and she's equipped with another cup of tea and a bowl of strawberries with cream to keep her going.

I'll give tonight an eight point five on the 'DOD' scale, my heart still fluttering from the risk of her taking a liking to the great outdoors again.

Still, she appears to be settled and that's all that matters right now.

19. Quieter and Quieter

In a perkier moment earlier, Mum looks out at the sky, telling me about the patches of blue that she saw earlier and how they're getting covered now with 'hazy, lazy clouds' again.

Otherwise, apart from the delightful hour she spent with Belinda, Mum's been at a fairly low ebb, her voice on its quietest setting, her hearing aids out and her usual *joie de vivre* out of reach somewhere, temporarily lost like so many other things.

I made a casserole this morning and popped it in the slow cooker ready for tonight. By dinnertime Mum was not far off lying horizontally on the settee, her legs out in front of her into the room, her arms lay loosely by her side and her eyes looked heavy, as though even looking at the sky was too much work.

The pattern was similar all day apart from when Belinda came and Mum made a special effort to sit upright. She fell asleep immediately after her breakfast. She held tightly on to the cup, itself balanced on the tray, and her head flopped down like a puppet without the strings.

Numerous cups of tea got delivered, then went cold, then got renewed throughout the day, each time Mum was only just able to muster the strength to look up, as though turning her head was way too much.

It's on days like these when I'm on higher alert, listening out, as I potter, for the slightest call from her. The best I got today was a "Fred?" when the postman arrived, other than that she's been either recharging her batteries or running them down further ready for recharging.

I dug out a copy of *Call the Midwife* for her to read. It's one that she's doubtless read many moons ago, but now appears to her to be a 'brand new book', ready to be devoured when the energy returns, as hopefully it will.

I sat with Mum before I served her meal, her body still laid out flat as though she'd fallen from a great height. I held her hand and wondered if she'd ever get her energy back. It's one of the many balancing acts involved, wondering if there'll be an abrupt end to our time together or if we still have many moons to go.

Being the eternal optimist with realistic tendencies, I opt for the former option of many moons to go, only with a side order of 'realistic proviso' that acknowledges how every day is a gift anyway, so be ready to accept whatever happens and whenever that may be.

Mum can't make it to the table to eat, even with the offer of the 'two-handed Martin lift', where I lift her up from the settee and her feet slide along the floor as she's so light. Her meal is subsequently served on a tray. Dessert followed after I'd called home.

The usual questions about who was joining us for tea lasted a few brief moments, too tired she was to even go through the regular routine that's preceded nearly every meal since April last year. There's no desire for TV, there's a book and a magazine close to hand if the energy returns, and otherwise Mum is happy with some 'shush'.

I must confess, I'm happy with some 'shush' too, but I daren't say so out loud, just in case it gets misconstrued.

So here's to some 'shush'… a welcome contrast to the frenetic times!

20. Rainy Days and Mondays

"Hanging around,

Nothing to do but frown,

Rainy days and Mondays always get me down."

Well actually they don't, and technically it's a Thursday, but none the less I'm stood at the kitchen sink, the rain's pouring down outside and I hear this old Carpenters song echoing through my mind, whisking me back to the 1970s when we were living at the big house on Chester Road.

The Carpenters appear in many a childhood memory, the rich sound of Karen Carpenter's lead vocal and Richard's orchestration, the lead guitar in *Goodbye to Love*, Dad smoking his pipe and listening to his eclectic record collection in the lounge, my brother and I playing board games or Lego, Mum in the kitchen forever cooking.

Back to the now and Mum's having a 'don't know where anything is' day so we've been like the automaton figures in a Black Forest clock, going in and out of rooms and in and out of rooms.

I lay Mum out a red jumper and some navy blue trousers on her bed to wear, then there's the missing underwear that's not really missing, just newly washed and dried and ready on her chair to go back into cupboards and drawers.

"I was wearing that jumper yesterday," says Mum.

"That was another red jumper Mum," I say and quickly hobble, due to my pulled back, to the lounge to get the one she cast off last night sometime between midnight and 5.00am.

"Oh, well I'll wear this one instead," she says, still completely lost as to where she is and where her clothes are.

Last night was a whole other story of Mum wanting to go home, a story that lasted from dinnertime to bedtime, a story that had Mum in her time machine with no way back to the now.

I head back to the kitchen and leave Mum to get dressed again, third time lucky I think to myself. My hands dip back into the soapy water, Radio 4's on in the background, though I know it will probably cause confusion at some point and sure enough Mum appears again in the hallway, talking to me in whispers from a distance in a voice that nobody could hear.

"Is that the radio?" Mum asks on the third attempt to get her voice above the whisper setting.

"Yes, we're on to *Woman's Hour* now Mum," I say, laughing at the role reversal from son to parent-carer-cum-butler.

"I thought I heard the lady who owns this place!" Mum says as we dance again to the constantly inconsistent dance of dementia.

Mum heads to the lounge again, still wearing her dressing gown and still confused by the actual process of getting dressed. It's not an everyday confusion, just one that when it arrives has to be met with patience and lots of repetition.

Dishes washed, I focus for a while on the making of tonight's dinner in the slow cooker. Mum is now enjoying another cup of tea while she gathers her faculties, so the coast is clear enough to lose myself once more in the time machine.

'Pink Floyd's *Dark Side of the Moon* is playing on my old record player upstairs at Chester Road, I'm making Airfix models, the smell of glue and Humbrol paint, the sound of Pink Floyd filling the room, tiny, tiny details getting painted with an extra-fine brush and I don't even need glasses! Mum's upstairs making the beds, Dad's in the lounge reading his paper, Rob's playing the piano in the front room and in the quieter passages of the Pink Floyd record I hear his own melodic notes come up through the floor from the room below.'

I've found that as I get older I've become more and more adept at using the time machine and can quite comfortably flit from now to then and back in the blink of an eye.

The slow cooker now filled with par-cooked ingredients, I grab the Dyson vacuum and clean the edges of the kitchen ready for a mopping later. As I turn off the vacuum I hear Mum calling out from the lounge:

"What's that noise?"

I hobble in with the vacuum to show her what I'm doing.

"Oh don't bother with that, I'll do that later," she says.

The truth is she's never once used this Dyson vacuum cleaner and it's been here three years now on a bracket by the door, but to Mum housework is something she still does every day.

"You've done your fair share of housework over the years Mum," I say in an attempt to shift the burden of the chores from her mind.

"Oh, I suppose I have, but I'm still the housewife of this house!" she insists.

"You have a butler these days, so let's leave it to him?" I suggest.

And Mum looks out of the window again, enjoying the Tupperware sky and the warmth of her gas fire.

"What I feel has come and gone before,

No need to talk it out,

We know what it's all about,

Hanging around,

Nothing to do but frown,

Rainy days and Mondays always get me down."

The Carpenters start to play in my mind's ear again, the smell of cooking wafts from the kitchen, the rain clatters on the conservatory roof, Mum's roasting nicely by the fire and the eternal now of 1970-something merges seamlessly with a rainy day in December 2018.

Blessings counted once more.

21. Low Ebb

"I've not felt this weak for years," says Mum, her voice as weak as weak can be.

I sit with her, hold her hand and describe, reassuringly, how her energy levels have dipped before and how plenty of rest has brought them back. She smiles, trusting my observations and willing herself to battle on.

Mum was late up this morning, in spite of the general 'getting up noises' I made, the turning on of the radio in the kitchen, the boiling of the kettle, the clink of plates going from the drainer back into cupboards.

At 10.00am Mum surfaced, albeit slowly. I'd heard her breathing the deep breaths of dreamy sleep earlier so knew she was OK in the dark of her room. She emerged from her bedroom holding her handbag, wearing her dressing gown and struggling to stay upright by the look of things.

I fetched her walking stick to help her steady herself. I could have easily just offered her an arm or a hand and walked her to the lounge, but the thought of the times when I'm not there remind me to keep on encouraging her belief in her independence.

She walks tentatively to the lounge, I watch her from a few paces back to make sure she's OK. She lands, rather than sits, in her favourite chair, the curtains already open to the world, and the morning sky is shades of blue streaked with soft tinted clouds.

Yesterday we'd had one last attempt at her Christmas card list, three pages of A4. But Mum just kept going in ever decreasing circles, unsure who to select, what to do or how to get beyond the thoughts to the actuality.

I sat up last night and completed the task, each card had a copy of her 'Christmas love and best wishes' that I'd photocopied and printed out, and then cut up into little rectangles of Mum's writing and stuck inside each card. I'd then addressed each envelope and put a name to each card. The walk out to the post box a welcome bit of fresh air as Mum rested in the warmth of her lounge.

Back home again, in the lamplight of my room I realise I'm now covered in glitter from the Christmas cards. A quick check in the bathroom mirror shows the glitter's not only on my T-shirt and trousers but also sparkling all over my hands and face. Ah well.

Despite the added sparkle, there's something strangely satisfying with completing a task, even if it's someone else's task; the reward is in the completion, even if the thoughts prior to the actual 'doing' are daunting and tainted with 100 ideas of useless procrastination.

Mum will have known this feeling on countless occasions, when she sat sewing labels into our clothes, darning our socks, washing and putting away our clothes or making our meals over the years. She will have also felt the reward of knowing she'd done all she could in each particular moment to allow our experience of growing up to be as good as it was.

I could almost predict a low ebb to today, given the way in which I got her to bed without any trouble last night and the fact she went straight to bed, 'did not pass Go and did not collect £200'.

It's unusual to experience a quiet night with no kitchen capers, no switching on and off and on of lights, no creaking of the front door or knocks at my door at all hours.

Doubtless Mum will build up her energy levels once more, turning from frail pensioner to feisty 'Bootle Lass' before you can say 'Jack Robinson', but in the meantime, I can catch my own breath, plan a few more meals, wrap a present or two, whip round with the duster once more.

David, the vicar, is coming to see Mum on Thursday afternoon so hopefully she'll have enough energy to appreciate his visit. Right now she's eating her neatly cut, triangular sandwiches with the crusts cut off, the plate covered in cling film once more to preserve what she can't eat in the first half hour.

Funnily, in these periods when she's at a low ebb, Mum returns, her head less busy and confused, her gentle nature to the forefront, and I'm grateful for the role I have as live-in butler to M' Ladyship.

Sssshhh now, Mum's resting!!

22. Batteries Fully Charged

After lunch Mum came alive. It took me five attempts just to complete making the bed.

"What should I do with this?" asks Mum, carrying a houseplant from the lounge.

"Do you want this?" she asks, presenting me with an old note for the milkman.

"My hearing aids won't stay in," she says, distantly from the hallway.

"What does this card say?" Mum asks, for the umpteenth time with the same card.

"Is this present from Doreen?" she asks, about to unwrap the present I'd wrapped this morning and left on the side ready to go out later.

Luckily for me David the vicar came early and gave me enough time to complete the task of making the bed. Now he's gone though Mum has been into the back room where I'm attempting to sort out a 'mixed bag of stuff' she presented me with earlier.

"Who is this card from?" asks Mum, bringing each of the cards from the lounge one by one (that's rather a few trips by the way).

"Where are you having your tea?" Mum asks, after her seventh knock already since the vicar left.

"Why does this card say To Robin?" Mum asks bringing me a now opened Christmas card that had been left for Robin on the sideboard.

"What shall we do about tea?" Mum asks on another uncontrollable urge to pace the hallway, forgetting she'd already witnessed the chilli in the slow cooker and declared how much her Mum likes this now.

"Are you here for tea tonight?" she asks, after another walk there and back.

"He's a lovely chap the vicar isn't he?" she states, as an excuse for another knock-knock.

"What are those?" Mum asks, seeing the contents of the bag she gave me earlier being sifted through like a customs man would at Gatwick Airport.

"What shall I do with these?" asks Mum after a whole five minutes of quiet where you know something's occurring but you're not sure what exactly. She's holding the now cut-off leaves from last year's amaryllis that she's kept all year afloat in an overfilled 'pot in a pot' I keep emptying into the sink when she's not looking.

I break off to take the leaves to the green bin and Mum says, "I didn't know we had a green bin!" and she follows me out to watch me place said leaves into said bin.

Selfishly I'd hoped for a relatively quiet evening so I can nip out and deliver some Christmas presents. At this rate though I may need to borrow a running machine from somewhere, set it to stroll and pop Mum on it to help wear her batteries back down a tad (he says, like the cartoon Coyote imagining all manner of ways to steal five minutes to himself).

Anyway, got to dash, there's rice to cook and a hungry Mum about to head down the hall again for round 20!

PS: I bet she won't want her dinner, I keep hearing the sound of the lid coming off the biscuits Doreen brought her and the crinkling of the paper inside the tin! Eh, what it's like being a parent to a parent!

23. Another Day

"Morning has broken, like the first morning,

Blackbird has spoken, like the first bird."

There it goes again, Cat Stevens' voice sings out in Martin's 'instant find-a-tune to fit any occasion' machine... I think to myself, as the relief of seeing Mum still breathing lifts me up once more.

As I got up this morning, I saw the light was still on in the lounge where I'd tucked Mum in last night and so I carried out the usual morning curtain opening duties. On goes the kettle, off goes the hall light, on goes the radio, and off goes the lamp in Mum's bedroom. It's become a well-rehearsed routine on quieter days, when all the circumstances align in the right order.

Quite naturally, given Mum's health and considerable years, there's always the lingering thought that this is the day when I find she's departed for the afterlife, but these thoughts are constantly countered by this boy's hopes, balanced with the adult-like acceptance of 'whatever will be'.

I bring Mum another cup of tea and place it beside her. She's still fast asleep, surrounded by all manner of things to read, the reading lamp still on, the fire burbling away and warming the room to a suitable heat for a seasonal hibernation.

Mum doesn't move, her hands still holding the recipe for North Staffordshire Oatcakes, not even the sound of me replacing the hot chocolate for a cup of tea makes her stir. You can just make out the tiny movements of her chest as she breathes the shallow breaths of a deep nocturnal slumber.

Contented with the medical assessment made by Dr Martin, I return to the kitchen for a pot of coffee, a slice of toast and some Radio 4 to assure myself that the world is still turning somewhere out there.

I return to the lounge to see Mum moving the books and making ready to greet the new day. This is the part where all my appreciation for the moment kicks in, a tear or two of thanks gathers in the corner of my eyes as I'm able to help Mum up from the settee and walk her with tiny, slow, unsteady steps to the loo.

Her walking stick's still in her bedroom, so I'll have to do instead, and even though I like to encourage her to keep using her own motor skills, this is one of those moments to savour, Mum and son in a full role reversal from 50 plus years ago. I sit down to finish my coffee and Mum asks if I've had my breakfast. She says she can get her own, so I listen as she heads off to the kitchen. Less than a few minutes later, after she's fully assessed the reality of the intention meeting the actual task, Mum returns to ask again if I've had any breakfast.

I've grown to love these subtle cues, the ones where questions about my wellbeing actually call for assistance, disguised in a secret parental coded language only detectable by the most attentive of sons and daughters, he says laughing to himself at the discovery.

I head to the kitchen and before Mum's followed me into the room, the cornflakes are in the bowl, the milk's out of the fridge and the tray's on the top with the sugar and a spoon at the side, ready for the milk to warm in the microwave.

Mum watches with that kind of motherly pride she once had when I stacked maybe four or so coloured wooden blocks on top of each other as a tiny child. It's either that or utter frustration of her now lost abilities to find all the components for any meal in this strange place she used to know as her home.

Mum recognises the tray and says, "We must remember to take those trays when we go home."

I imagine that these trays are ingrained upon her memory in spite of everything, thanks to the golden years of living here with Dad before he died in 2015. Breakfast, lunch and dinner (tea) will have been served on these trays and of all things in the house these have somehow survived the ravages of vascular dementia.

I guide Mum back to the lounge, the curtains now open, the reading lamps off, her cushions fluffed and help her down again into her command seat in the 'Starship Enterprise' to once more enjoy a breakfast while looking out into the realms of outer space. Well OK, a suburban scene blanketed in milky clouds and daylight that theoretically masks the actual stars, but we still know they're there, Mum and I, two intrepid travellers through space and time.

And so, fellow space travellers, here we are once more, thank goodness, boldly going into another day!

24. Breakfast in Bed

"Breakfast In Bed, Kisses For Me ..." goes the UB40 song in my head, only it's 11.00pm, I'm miles away from home and Mum's ready for her breakfast.

These dark mornings and long dark nights have thrown Mum's body clock into disarray. She likes a nap at the best of times, but a nap can easily be confused with a full night's sleep if you don't know where you are or what time it is.

I go along with the storyline, preparing Mum's breakfast tray at 11.00pm as though it's actually morning. I say to myself 'why not?' it's only like supper anyway. I take advantage of the late hour as an excuse to get to bed myself and prepare the lounge for Mum so she can sleep in her chair once she's had her nocturnal breakfast.

Somehow, I sleep then until 5.00am without any disturbance and lie there pondering life and the universe until 7.00am, when I hear the first stirrings from the lounge as Mum goes to open and close the front door a few times.

"Did the doorbell wake you too?" asks Mum.

"Yes Mum!" I fib, just to go along with the story.

Mum goes one way up the hall and I head the other to make a start on breakfast.

It's amazing how long Mum can go without food, I suppose it's because she's not burning it off, pacing the hall or walking with me on a prom somewhere, as we did in summer. This morning though, two cups of tea held on to but not even sipped and at least three offers of cereal for breakfast have all been rejected. She's happy, watching the clouds, as I guess I would be too given the circumstances.

My brother Rob and I have both scoured the house for the two sets of salt and pepper pots that went missing a couple of weeks ago now, not a sign. Also on the missing articles list is a pack of salmon steaks, intended for last night's dinner, plus of course, the elusive sugar bowl.

Mum called me in earlier to ask about the milkman.

"Martin?" she calls from the lounge to the kitchen.

"Yes Mum?" I reply, moving fairly rapidly based on the sound of urgency in her voice.

"The milkman has been and left me a bottle of milk this morning!" she says with a mixture of astonishment and surprise.

"Yes, he comes here every couple of days," I reply, hoping it will help.

"Oh, I didn't know that!" she says, still trying to fathom the mystery.

This leads me to check the fridge, where there's no sign of the fresh milk Mum had mentioned earlier. I check all the cupboards and eventually find the bottle of milk, nicely warming to room temperature in the cupboard under the sink.

I get back to the task of pondering Mum's calls to her butler. In the old stately homes the servants used to respond to a series of bells in the kitchen when the Lady of the house called. I wonder about the practicality of such a contraption, well the bells and perhaps a series of pipes with a mouthpiece at Mum's end and earpieces throughout the house for good measure. The only downside to such an arrangement is we're only in a tiny bungalow so maybe an old-fashioned megaphone would suffice?

Mum calls again from the lounge…

"Martin?"

"Yes Mum?" I reply, remembering the days when I used to skid in my socks on the polished floor of the old house (I used to love doing that!).

"What are these?" she asks, pointing to the dark spots on the lounge carpet.

"It's just where drinks have been spilt and dust has stuck," I reply, hoping the reply was clear enough.

"We'll have to shampoo the carpet," I add for good measure.

Mum studies the dark spots and goes into silent mode while she processes the situation. I head back to the kitchen to carry on with whatever it was I was doing only to hear another call from the lounge…

"Martin?"

"Yes Mum?" I reply, this time responding at less than an urgent pace.

"What are those two eyes over there?"

"Oh, that's the Ringtons Tea Box," I reply, while going to fetch the box to show her.

"Sing some sea fox?" Mum answers, the words now reinterpreted through her universal translator.

"Ringtons – Tea – Box," I try again, while busily opening it up to reveal a series of contents like something off the QVC shopping channel.

The dementia has this unfortunate effect of scrambling what Mum sees and hears and experiences for that matter, so in this case, the shiny foiled blue gift box with stars on it, a Christmas present, was seen as two peering eyes from far across the room as it reflected the light from the window.

I imagine the perfect environment for dementia sufferers would be a minimalist home, one where every bit of clutter was hidden away and only a small selection of treasured objects was on view. Then again, that wouldn't be the home Mum's used to, so maybe a constant scaling down of clutter is the compromise… less is more, as they say.

Anyway, I'll have to dash, Mum's just called out my name again… hold that thought!

25. Silence of the Mams

I'm guessing, well hoping, it's the same for many carers, that there are times when it all goes quiet, where the confusion, anxiety and stress of the dementia sufferer all fade away for a while and a calm comes over them.

It's one such day today with Mum. Early to rise as usual, though positively subdued in her demeanour from yesterday. Happy in herself, content with the view from her chair, delighted to be brought breakfast, drinks or lunch, or simply to read her book.

I've got loads done, prepared a meal for later, made fresh fruit salad, tightened all the screws on the pans and their lids, I even changed the tablecloth and cleared the strand of clutter and debris that had washed up there on the incoming tide over recent weeks.

Mum made at least four separate attempts to get washed and dressed. Each one started with an official declaration of intent. Each one interrupted by different distractions, from nails that needed filing to a rediscovered letter from America.

Like any of us, Mum doesn't like to be hurried, she prefers to get wherever she's going in her own good time, which makes getting out of the door before mid afternoon these days a chore and a half.

It may have been the warrior like exertions of yesterday that have resulted in a sedate pace to this morning, it may equally be normal for the anxieties to ebb and flow from one day to the next.

I'll keep this short, so we can all enjoy the quiet after the storm, the peace after the battles we all face from time to time.

Here's to calm and all who sail on her.

26. Not Confetti?

Every Christmas for as long as I can remember, Mum and Dad used to put cryptic clues on the gift tags to everyone's presents. I think perhaps they would have approved of the title to this missive, especially given the circumstances.

I had to leave Mum last night to attend to something back home in Yorkshire. I had dinner with Mum first and left some rice in a sieve, resting in an empty pan and with a lid on it to keep any bugs off it.

Tonight, while making a repeat of last night's dinner, I again made a pan of rice and noticed the sieve was now on top of the pan rack, its normal 'ready for action' place being a hook on the right of the pan rack.

I thought to myself 'how's Mum got that up there?' and reached it down to sieve the rice once it had boiled. It was like being married, you know, that part where the bride and groom get showered in rice after the wedding? Only in this case, there was only me, no guests and no lych gate for that matter!

It's surprising just how far a little rice can go, and luckily for me, Mum was busy setting the table otherwise she would have had it in her hair, especially given how her default standing position when I'm cooking is right in close so she can see what's going on.

Also luckily for me, the rice was dry now it had been baked in the ambient dryness of central heating since whenever Mum put it up there. In any normal kind of situation one would be entitled to ask why anyone had put a sieve with rice in it on top of a pan rack; however, these are extraordinary circumstances and Mum would deny any knowledge of it anyway! In truth I'd be in trouble for even asking!

A few years ago I installed a Dyson vacuum cleaner on the wall in the hallway, easy for an elderly parent to use, lightweight enough to manage and constantly charged up ready for the inevitable spillages that occur in the home.

I'm sure Mum thinks about hoovering quite often, but she's possibly been wary of the Dyson and prefers it instead when I whizz around the lounge with it, she even lifts her feet up so I can hoover around her, just like I did no doubt when I was a teenager.

The wedding rice didn't drop into tonight's rice, even though it was below it on the hob. It did however get everywhere else and into some hard to reach places too, hopefully I got it all, but you never know with such things!

When Mum came back to see if I needed any more help, the hoovering was done, the rice was nearly ready and the dinner all ready to go straight from the slow cooker to our plates. They say 'ignorance is bliss'… well at least that's exactly what Dad would have said in the circumstances.

Talking of weddings, Mum had a lovely couple of hours yesterday with a new volunteer carer, Belinda, who I'd first met 35 years ago when some mutual friends got married. Belinda was the chief bridesmaid and I was the best man. Such is the power of social media to reconnect us with friends we'd otherwise lose track of.

It transpires that Belinda had experience of being a carer, and whilst Mum sees quite a number of carers and has done since Dad died, for Mum this was more like a friend coming round to spend time with her, and you could see this from the way Mum's face lit up during and afterwards from the quality time they had together.

Overall, apart from the occasional glitches, Mum appears to be much happier in herself this week, a little more accepting of the lack of missing relatives at meal times and generally a bit steadier on her feet than she has been for a while.

Right now she's tucking into a little bowl of bananas and cream, a treat she used to love in the good old days and one I distinctly recall being served in little stainless steel bowls for 'afters' but then again my own memories are beginning to cloud in some areas.

Sorry, Mum's calling again so I'd better dash!

Quick, where's my butler's hat?

27. A New Book

Mum's delight in receiving the new book was evident, especially with it being about Chester where she lived after the war and before moving to Poynton. Of course we've had many a new book over recent times and the joy of receiving them for the first time never seems to diminish for Mum.

It's nice to land on anything that brings light relief to the merry-go-round of dementia symptoms and I'm sure it's different for everyone. In Mum's case, memories of her younger life seem to work best, any mention of Liverpool or Bootle or Crosby or Tarporley or Chester and she lights up with the instant connection to something she knows to be true.

The house is filled with cooking smells. Mum's got herself dressed, got a few of the familiar things back on her side table and enjoyed a breakfast earlier of toast and marmalade. The radio is on in the kitchen, all the dishes are put away and the slow cooker is filled with tonight's meal simmering away. In fact, it's the perfect 'homely' scene for Mum to relax and escape the anxieties that come with not knowing where you are or where everyone else is.

She really must be tired, I'm tired and I'm 35 years younger. Last night was another battle with the bedtime routine. I made the hot chocolate at 10.00pm, turned everything off or down in the lounge, her bedside lamp on, curtains closed, walking stick to hand, said our goodnights then off to bed myself.

Ten minutes later and Mum's stumbling into the darkness of my room to say goodnight again, as though it's for the first time. She leaves my door wide open and heads off to get ready for bed. I get out of bed, close my door and listen for the hoped-for silence.

I wonder if a similar routine occurred when Dad was alive, the one where Mum paces the hall, plays with light switches in the lounge and the kitchen, opens and closes the front door, makes herself a collection of drinks to go with her hot chocolate? It must have been so tough for Dad, witnessing Mum losing her faculties one by one like this.

I hear the Poynton church bells strike midnight as the final shuffles to bed are heard heading into Mum's room.

I have tried on a number of occasions helping Mum get to bed, these have all failed as when there's an anxiety about something it's difficult to take it away, even with TLC and oodles of assurance. So I'm resigned to dancing with this situation for the foreseeable, letting Mum do what she needs to do in her own good time.

I wish in a way that there were still matrons like there used to be in the 'good old days', the matriarchs that everyone respected and feared in equal measure. If there were, I'd hire one at bedtime every night to get Mum tucked in and ready for lights out. I imagine this would work, especially given how the little girl in Mum has often come out to play mischief while I've been here.

Anyway, today's a new day, the homely feel to the house today and the obvious delight with the new book suggest it will be a good one, a day where Mum can relax, enjoy a trip down memory lane and see the world passing by her window.

Right then, time for lunch! Salmon sandwich anyone?

28. Take it or Leave it?

Mum points to the treasured collection on the windowsill, digging deep to find the words to go with the thought she wants to express. It's along the lines of "I'd like to take that one and that one with me when we go," which tells me the idea of this being a 'temporary visit' is still a predominant one.

With a little pair of scissors, she carefully cuts off any dead leaves from the two pot plants near the window, collecting the cut-off pieces in her hand to go into the bin.

"That's George and Doreen Mum," I say, filling in a long silent gap as she tried unsuccessfully to remember the names of people in a photograph.

"Oh, is that who it is?" she exclaims, both surprised and confused in equal measure.

"I've not seen them in years," she continues, her eyes fixed on the blue sky, the place she looks for answers during the daytime.

"It was your wedding anniversary when you last saw George," I say, pointing to another photo of Mum and Dad's Diamond Anniversary.

"Gosh, was it that long ago?" Mum asks, not sure how long ago that was or what year it is now.

I did the usual check around as I arrived this Monday morning, nothing seemed out of place, no raw food in the cupboards at least.

We enjoyed a nice cuppa together as Mum tried to explain how the neighbours' gardens were related by similar ideas but how one had worked out better than the other.

The overarching thought or observation today was how quiet it was and how it felt like a Sunday. The idea came to me about putting a bird feeder near her window and that way she could at least see the little birds once more that gave her so much enjoyment over summer.

I ventured to the kitchen for a quick stock check before doing the shopping and noticed an unusual fan sound, whirring away from somewhere. It's not the boiler I thought and my eyes went straight to the oven, one of the knobs was slightly turned to one of the settings other than 'off'. There was no heat luckily, but on opening the door there was a surprise…

A plate with an uneaten sandwich, a dollop of coleslaw, a handful of crisps and a side order of used teabags in its own cling film wrapper. It was obviously the remnants of something made for her as one of the new regime changes with the carers is to make 'snacky' type meals and leave them covered up for when Mum's hungry. Mum's default thought is 'feeding everyone else' hence this got left for whoever came in next and needed feeding.

Right now, Mum's enjoying some crosswords again, it's amazing she can recall the words let alone translate the clues, but the brain is a remarkable thing. She's also got a new book or two to read, given to her one at a time to avoid overload, and I've just cleared away last week's collection of books, bits of wrapping paper, empty picture frames and newspapers that somehow gather on her sofa like flotsam and jetsam do on a deserted beach.

Talking of beaches and the things that we find there, Mum has some tiny seashells, maybe kept from a holiday long ago when Dad was alive. She's placed these on the corner of the oak casket that holds Dad's ashes, like a secret acknowledgement of his passing that in turn reaches out a hand to the idea he's still here with us. Just like an open hand with the shells you'd collect and show a loved one, just as you did as a child and just as in awe now as you were then at the timeless nature of the sea.

Perhaps, behind the dementia she knows he's gone now, but prefers to live out old scenarios, ones where we were both here as younger men, where Dad was in the other room, where everyone she knew was just a letter or a phone call away.

I don't suppose we'll ever really know how the world looks now for Mum, the best we can do is 'go with,' and 'be with,' and perhaps also, that's all she wants anyway?

29. Not Counting Sheep

"I'm so tired, I haven't slept a wink,

I'm so tired, my mind is on the blink,

I wonder should I get up and fix myself a drink,

No, no, no."

John Lennon sings an impromptu verse from The Beatles' *White Album* though it's only me who can hear it. I smile to myself as I recall the days when I used to have stereo speakers set up either side of my teenage bed and I'd fall asleep listening to *Sergeant Pepper* or *The Magical Mystery Tour.*

Tonight I was preparing for a deep sleep; I'd read earlier about the importance of sleep and not looking at computer screens an hour before going to bed. The stage was set, I'd followed the instructions and was relishing the thought of establishing a new healthy night time routine. Mum had her hot chocolate, the fire in the lounge was turned down to its tiny pilot light, the lights were off, Mum was in her bedroom getting herself ready for bed and it all seemed to be going perfectly to plan.

I'm sure as you're reading this you're already thinking this is all going to go horribly wrong and not wishing to disappoint, here's what happened next.

It all goes quiet, so quiet all I could hear was the sound of my breathing and the central heating pipes expanding and contracting. The near pitch-darkness of my room is only punctured here and there through chinks in the curtain or a little light from the hall seeping under the bedroom door.

I begin to drift, you know, that way when you can feel yourself heading off in the right direction but you're still aware of your surroundings? Then there's the void, where you drift off into the dream world and you become unaware that you're asleep, you simply are.

FUMBLE, RATTLE, KNOCK, Mum enters the room and the long anticipated sleep is broken…

"What should I do with the fire?" asks Mum.

"It's off Mum, I turned it off, it's OK now," I say, fully conscious now.

"Oh, OK, night-night love, sweet dreams," she says once more and I'm more awake than I was before I went to bed.

I lie there once more, listening intently, rubbing my eyes, wondering, imagining.

No sounds, it's all gone quiet, I flip the pillow to find a cool spot, get comfy and prepare for the recently delayed sleeper train to 'Sleep-Ville'.

Even though I'm still listening intently while simultaneously attempting to prepare for sleep, I fail to hear Mum magic herself from her bedroom to the bathroom. She flushes the loo with gusto, it sounds twice as loud at night somehow. There's an ominous creek on the floorboard outside my door and…

FUMBLE, RATTLE, KNOCK, Mum enters the room

"What should I do with the fire?" asks Mum.

I'll fast forward at this point, so if you can imagine the film speeding up, my sleepy head bobbing up and down, on and off the pillow, Mum entering the room, then exiting again, then going to bed then getting up, entering the room, then going to bed again, almost like something from an old Benny Hill comedy sequence.

Six times Mum entered the room after the apparent silence of going to bed, six times she asked the same question in slightly different ways, the last of which suggested that Dad used to unplug it before bedtime, which is quite strange as they'd always had a gas fire, unless of course she's going right back to the old days of a five-bar electric fire… anyway, six times!!

It was now 00.30am; we'd started the bedtime routine at 10.00pm. I lay there in the darkness and imagined I was in a Laurel and Hardy scene. I'm Oliver Hardy and looking directly at the camera, Stan Laurel is fast asleep in the other room. I'm lying there with wide-open, bloodshot eyes and fiddling with the collar on my stripy pyjamas. I can see it now.

I did eventually get off to sleep, Mum did get up early again this morning and the night felt a tad shorter than I'd hoped for, but hey, tonight's another night!

30. Ghosts of Futures Past

Mum emerges from the lounge, she stands in the darkness, wondering. I hear her come out into the hall so I head from my room to meet her and see if she's all right.

"Ssh, your Dad's asleep now," she says, looking back into the lounge.

"Is he in there now Mum?" I ask excitedly, wishing he'd manifest himself somehow.

"Yes, he's right there," she says, pointing to his chair and realising his physical self is now no longer there.

"I feel so stupid, I've just been talking to him," she adds, and I believe her.

How can you be with someone for 63 years and not feel their presence everywhere you go? Or not talk to them after they're gone like you did for a lifetime?

It's been a low energy day today, although it had early promises of being another frenetic one as Mum had already got her coat and bag ready to go out again, only this time it was to her Tuesday group, something she used to do a couple of years ago when her morning routine was more accommodating and the weather more spring-like.

I whisked away the coat she'd left on a chair at the dining table and hid it away in case seeing it made her think again of heading out into the cold. Distractions and books and just sitting with her watching the birds and the sky did the trick and eased away the re-run thoughts of yesteryear.

I even made it out to the shops for light bulbs and to the chemist to get some magnesium tablets and lavender spray for her pillow to help with the sleeping routine. She watched me from the lounge window as I de-iced the car and made ready for the road. A food bag filled with warm water melted away the ice on the frosted-up windscreen, a scraper for the thicker ice and hey presto, all done.

On my return, Mum was exactly where I'd left her, comfy in the lounge, sat in her favourite chair, warm and toasty from the fire, a cup of tea in one hand and her book of Liverpool in her lap, her eyes transfixed on the pages within.

I made her lunch a bit later, ate mine at the table and she continued with her book. Her lunch got half eaten but at least she had something, I thought.

By dinner time I'd made a meal for tomorrow night and a different one for tonight. I set the table and helped Mum up, walking her, hesitant step by hesitant step, to the table, her balance letting her down once more.

She toyed with her meal but only ate a few new potatoes before declaring her lack of appetite in that moment. I helped her back to her chair and brought her a fresh cup of tea to drink while I called home.

There's a carer with her now. Mum's in her 'quiet mode' so just listening as the young carer chats away to her and adds, I'm sure, the much-needed female company to today's mix.

To a casual observer, compared to yesterday, anyone would think it was a different person sat in the lounge today. She's been delighted to see me each time I've checked in on her, she's been engrossed in her book and loved every page so far and our conversations have been about everyday things she sees from her window.

Yesterday I was 'a horror' and the focus of her symptomatic anger from dawn till dusk. My secret though is the love she taught me as a boy and nothing could ever dim that light.

Well, we made it through another day unscathed Dad, if you're reading this, I saw you today, disguised as the sunlight reflecting on the snowy lawn near Mum's window.

Miss you Dad!

31. Standing Around

As frenetic days go, yesterday was a long one. The carer was due at 8.00pm and got delayed in a roadblock after a car crash, luckily a police officer let her through.

By 8.40pm I finally sat down for a break.

Just prior to this I found myself standing around, waiting near the front door, thinking to myself that it was pointless to go and sit down as the carer would be here any minute. So I stood and I stood.

Earlier with Mum I'd sat and I'd sat. Earlier still we stood and we stood and we stood some more. In fact, we broke our record today for standing. Lounge, conservatory, bedroom, kitchen and hallway, each got the standing treatment.

I'm sure it would look most strange if we were on CCTV, Mum and I just stood there, the long silent pauses as Mum digs deep for whatever it was that was niggling her, me waiting patiently, not putting words in her mouth, just giving her the space to express the thought, or not as is mostly the case.

Mum broke another world record after our evening meal; consecutive trips up the hallway from the kitchen to ask about tea, coffee or another evening meal, then church, then coffee then tea… nineteen trips in half an hour.

I made dinner earlier with Mum literally clung on to my side, in fact she's been alongside all day. The golden hour, where dementia sufferers play a daily memory loop, in Mum's case asking about meals around the same time each day, was truly golden, helped mostly by the winter skies and the last drips of golden sunlight that stream into the kitchen in late January afternoons.

Mum suddenly came over all panicked, would there be enough food for all the others, where are they all, how are we going to feed them all? Somehow I managed to change the topic or shift the focus on to setting the table and other such distractions, but the thought once present can't be un-thought and it stays with Mum for hours or sometimes days (as it did with the idea about moving house earlier this week).

Dinner finished, all the dishes washed and Mum settled with another cup of tea, I set off to call home from the conservatory. I left Mum in the lounge and closed three doors behind me just so I could have five minutes selfishly to myself.

I called home and got a whole five minutes before the door to the conservatory opened slowly and Mum came in. I cut short the call home and went back to the lounge with Mum for a sauna. Gee it's hot in there!

Mum's been refusing her hearing aids today so hearing me has been a further challenge, tonight though I put new batteries in and somehow persuaded her she would enjoy hearing things better. It worked.

The sad part for Mum on days like these are the moments where she experiences herself as being mentally lost. She hugs me, tells me she loves me and shares how she doesn't know what to do.

There were a few of these moments today and the last one was rare in that her eyes welled up with tears. It's something she hasn't done in years, not even when Dad died, it's almost as though at that point in her life the dementia was a momentary blessing as otherwise she'd have been heartbroken.

I suggest that the best medicine we know is a good book, one to absorb herself in and take her mind off things. After the tears we headed back to the lounge to find the latest book on Liverpool, one she could relate to and escape the 'now' for a while.

One of the things I've noticed with Mum's symptoms is how she can be angry and violent in one moment, then meek and mild the next, so being consistent as the carer/son/butler is vital. When I say consistent, I mean calm when she's angry and calm when she's tearful and calm when she's panicking. It may sound obvious, but the calmer I am, the quicker Mum's storms blow over and the quicker she returns to her own reflected calmness.

Once the relief carer had gone the evening progressed steadily downhill. Mum's determination to attend an imaginary funeral service at church was palpable.

"I'll get my coat," says Mum heading for the cupboard in the hall.

"It's very cold out there tonight and way too late for a church service," I suggest.

"I'll go myself if you don't want to go," she says, her frustration turning to anger.

It's now 9.40pm, the pavements are covered in frozen snow and Mum's not been out on her own for three years to my knowledge, so clearly a walk to church on her own is out of the question. I dig deep for the distractions to keep her warm and safe, but as they say 'Hell hath no fury like a Mum determined' and I have to be the 'bad guy' for finding umpteen ways to delay her exit into the cold night.

I stick to the plot and prepare the lounge for her to sleep in there, she's clearly not willing to consider going to bed, so I pretend she's not really sulking and bring her hot chocolate, a dressing gown and her blanket... just in case she decides to sleep in there. The plot worked, well, largely.

Using a small collection of available tools, I wedge the bedroom door shut so it can't be opened from the hallway, at this point I'm determined to get the full night's sleep I'd promised myself. I knew Mum was as safe as she could be and had access to anything she needed.

I lay there for a good couple of hours, listening just in case. The house was silent. I turned over and headed off to sleep at midnight. At 4.00am Mum's up and about, gets washed, then goes back to the lounge before rising once more at 7.00am when she must have thought it a good idea to try my door.

Rattle, rattle, fumble goes the door handle but the wedge holds fast and Mum gives up and retreats in silence once more to the lounge. I get up and dressed quickly to go and check on her.

I have to confess to enjoying early starts, well that was the case most of my working life, but I did get to bed at a decent time to give myself the energy for an early start. Caring for Mum demands the candle is burnt at both ends now, so the new motto is 'Late to bed and early to rise, and that was the cause of his early demise!'

Anyway, today's a whole new day and hopefully it's a whole different story!

32. Where Are We Now?

I hear David Bowie singing…

"Where are we now?

Where are we now?

The moment you know,

You know,

You know."

And I'm wondering where Mum thinks we are right now, or in any given moment, now I come to think of it.

Our brains are capable of experiencing thoughts of past and future moments as though they're 'here and now' and each relived or imagined moment can feel like a tangible reality.

Of all the things we do in a day, Mum seems happiest with books, especially those that whisk her back to a time and place where the memories are still as crisp and clear as they've always been.

Shorter-term memories have mostly been scrambled, dislodged, erased or darkened to the point she can no longer make sense of them. Her eyes see me but her brain turns the visual cues into someone else, as though other 'known faces' are being projected on to a manikin.

I've refilled the bird feeder with wild bird food this morning; it's catching the breeze and swaying near Mum's window. A reference sheet with pictures of Britain's wild birds provides something to talk about, to offer up as something to look out for or recognise from last summer in the back garden.

As children we'd play with something for a short while, then run out to play in the garden or climb trees or hide in spidery sheds and get coal dust on our clean clothes. Dad would refer to our short-lived enjoyment of these things as 'five minute wonders' and now I'm seeing the loop close back on itself.

Melancholy is the best word I can grasp to describe the quiet time Mum experiences in between the thoughts of who, what, where and when.

I wonder if 'melancholy' is actually a place somewhere in our collective minds, a place where we reflect upon the now intangible yet intentional 'could, should and would' moments of our days? Wherever it is or whatever it is, it's a constant place I see Mum going, a place that's only disturbed by distraction or the arrival of others be they friends, relatives or carers.

Yesterday was a busy day; Mum had company from Belinda after lunch, a visit from one of the relief care providers late afternoon, then a party to go to for her granddaughter at teatime and a young carer in the evening who stayed until 9.00pm.

By 10.00pm Mum was tired, so I made preparations towards the bedtime routine, hot chocolate, lights down low, dressing gown and blanket all ready. I also mentioned to Mum about keeping my door closed once I'd gone to bed and said that I'd put a note on the door to remind her. The note said 'Martin sleeping, night-night' and it said this deliberately to keep the message simple.

Mum did potter about until midnight, making umpteen drinks, midnight feasts and numerous trips up and down the hallway, but each time she approached my door, I could hear her stop in her tracks, read the note then head off to make yet another drink.

The upshot being that I'm no use to Mum if I'm dead on my feet from lack of sleep. Whilst I did stay awake until midnight listening out for Mum, she did, none the less, retire to her bedroom to sleep, a first time for a good while.

She was up, bright as a button this morning, happy to sit and watch the world go by her window and happier still cradling a cup of tea with the fire turned up to 'warp-factor-three'. Interestingly, the fire was turned down last night by Mum, which is surprising as she never usually touches it these days believing it to be a coal fire or seemingly afraid of getting it wrong.

I've asked Mum about where she goes in her mind and she tells me, "It's not a place I can describe, I can't find the words to describe it," and that's sadly the case for many things with dementia, the thoughts are there but the words get stuck somewhere.

Where are we now?

I'm guessing the answer to this is 'wherever our thoughts take us'.

Wherever you are Mum, I'm here.

33. The Red Jumper

The afternoon appeared to be going OK. Mum had spent an hour with Belinda and had a lovely time going through a load of old photos. Meanwhile I'd nipped out to the shops for a missing item or two.

I'm kicking myself now as I even had the thought 'Ooh, I wonder if the red jumper is a good idea?' but I carried on as Mum was in a fret about where her clothes were again.

"I can't find a vest," she said, frustrated with the whole thing about not knowing where anything is.

"You've got one on," I reply, assuring her I hoped.

"Not a vest, I mean trousers," Mum says, still struggling to identify what it is she wants. (On that note, I remembered how babies cry but can't communicate in words.)

"You've got trousers on Mum," I again assure her.

"Who keeps moving all my bloody clothes?" she asks.

"There's only you and me here Mum and your clothes won't fit me!" I joke to lighten the mood and Mum laughs.

I reach into the wardrobe and pull out the red jumper. Even Mum makes a noise as though to say, 'oh no, not the red jumper,' and unwittingly I create 'Muminstein' right there in her bedroom, without the aid of a single electrode.

Mid afternoon tea is served and you'd think Mum had taken several angry pills while I was in the kitchen.

"What's this?" she demanded as I handed her another cup of tea.

"A nice cup of tea Mum," I say, hoping it's just a blip.

"Oh, I see you've taken over in the kitchen now have you?" and I feel the spot lamp get turned on as my cheeks flush up from the heat of the interrogation.

I take a deep breath, smile and attempt to escape before I'm eaten alive.

Mum throws her hearing aids at me as I exit stage left.

I bring them back and put them on the table near the window, just out of reach for throwing again but safe enough and where they're needed.

I head back in to see Mum again about half an hour later and attempt some small talk. The red jumper has still taken over Mum like a demonic possession and she's unable to say anything without two pounds (or 907 grams) of venom thrown in for good measure.

"Have you seen any birds on the feeder today Mum?" I ask, as just one tiny example of the way these things can pan out.

"Never mind the bloody feeder, why's everything moved on the windowsill?" she asks, her hearing now miraculously cured.

"Sorry Mum, that's me, I cleaned the windowsill this morning while you watched," I reply, throwing in the circumstances just in case she's recording anything.

"You're bloody useless, no help at all!" she says, her eyes on fire and shafts of lightning about to set fire to the rug.

"One does one's best M' Ladyship," I say.

"Well your bloody best isn't good enough is it?" she says, in a way that may have done me good as a boy but is frankly wasted on me now that I'm 57.

I suggest I have some more chores to do and head off to still my beating heart, the butterflies in my stomach are having a field day and I wish there was a way to ease the confusion in her head. I'm at a loss though, so busy myself with the chores while the storm front from Bootle passes.

The making of dinner was even tougher. Mum was convinced she'd been ousted from her role of matriarch and chief cook and now resigned to following orders from me, the bloody butler of all people!

"What can I do?" asks Mum, not exactly in her best 'employ me I'll do a good job' voice, more of a going through the motions 'what can I do?'.

I give her fruit to work with, bananas, apples, tangerines and grapes. 'That should keep you happy' I thought as I pressed on with the evening meal. Mum drums her fingers on the worktop, a sure signal she's struggling with any given task. She stares at the fruit, willing it to move but it stays there, defying her seemingly indomitable will.

Mum gets a knife to cut a tangerine. I ask her if that's for tonight's afters. The knife heads my way, clattering against the cupboard, the tangerine gets flung at the kettle. Luckily the knife is relatively blunt and would only go in a few inches if it struck me, so I'm unscathed.

Mum heads to the lounge for a sulk. I carry on with the meal and attempt despite the butterflies to make a nice casserole.

Mum returns, nice as pie, butter wouldn't melt and you'd never even know there'd been any demonic possession at all. She hugs me and thanks me for making dinner and explains how her mind is all mixed up and how she feels useless.

"Mum, you're doing brilliantly," I say and of course I mean it as the subtleties of intonation are still well within Mum's grasp.

"Thank you love, you are too," she says, as though she's able to give witness to the symptoms whilst at the same time unable to stop them.

We sit down for our meal, a fight almost breaks out over the number of guests. When I say fight I mean Mum was about to lose her cool once more and I'd have just let it blow over, but to Mum it would have felt like a fight as she's both the aggressor and the witness at the same time.

Mum enjoys her meal followed by afters of raspberries and cream. I leave her to enjoy another cup of tea while I call home. I get a whole five minutes to myself before Mum's on the prowl once more. I cut short my call, then return to make Mum another cup of tea as the previous one isn't quite right (which is code for I need company or else).

Luckily for me, the relief carer is due earlier than usual tonight and will be with Mum for an hour to provide some much-needed female company. I can hear from where I'm sat that the carer's youthful energy is just what Mum needed and it sounds like she's still alive after 30 minutes so all is good.

Tomorrow I'll hide the red jumper and make sure there's a few other nice ones to choose from. I may even dig a pit in the garden, do some ritual incantations and burn the red jumper, sending its demonic properties back to wherever they came from.

Well, it's either that or call for a priest!

Joking aside, the symptoms of dementia can be hard to deal with for any carer. It's tougher still if it's a relative that's suffering, so all I can offer to Mum who's on the inside of this illness is that the storm will soon pass and she'll feel much better in a short while. Invariably she does.

That's the wonderful thing about unconditional love, it's unconditional and no matter what happens, it endures everything.

34. South Specific

Every now and then things align to make for a perfect moment.

This morning was a rare one indeed.

The sun shone. The skies were blue with low, distant clouds.

The lounge was dusted. The carpets vacuumed.

The windowsill shone a sparkling bright white.

Rainbows danced on as many surfaces as they could find, reflected from the little crystals that hang in the window bay.

Bright sparks of light glinted in a myriad of colours off the corners of picture frames on the windowsill. Photos of now-passed relatives seemed to smile even brighter.

Biscuits on a little plate for this morning's tablets, a cup of tea ready on the side table.

Dishes washed and put away, bins emptied, everything ship-shape and Bristol fashion.

We sat down, Mum and I.

"Which would you like Mum, South Specific, Carousel, Sound of Music, Gigi?" I asked, knowing she'd probably ask for the first one anyway.

"South Pacific I think?" says Mum, liking them all and not knowing which to choose for the best.

"South Specific it is then" I declare and duly pop the CD into the player.

Mum's ears take a while to tune into the opening track. I adjust the volume until it's just right and sit back to see how Mum responds.

She smiles from ear to ear and sings along to songs she recognises. Her smile is infectious and tears of momentary joy run down my cheeks. Mum can't see me, she's just looking towards the speaker, time-travelling to the era when she watched the musical on stage with Dad, back in the day.

Her fingers tap along to the rhythm, she knows all the words to the songs, she's happier than a child at Christmas and positively beaming.

There's a carer due at 11.30am so we'll revisit the 'Poynton West End Theatre' a bit later, maybe after lunch, but for now this is an audio-visual treat to savour. A moment I'll hold and look back on, one where Mum was positively aligned with a place in time where everything was just as it should be.

These moments are rare and treasured. Mum didn't take to the carer sadly and gave her short shrift. I imagine this was partly due to her arrival just in the middle of a favourite song. Still, the carers are used to being seen off the premises and Mum, reverting for a moment to her Bootle training, took no prisoners and gave no quarter!

Lunch next and a cheese butty should help to change the subject, maybe some more 'South Specific' later. For now though I'm still elated inside from Mum's happiness I witnessed earlier. And now that I know there's a way to reach it, then I imagine we'll be able to find it again.

Perhaps this is as good as it gets for anyone with this curse of an illness.

Duty calls.

35. The Missing Bedroom

It's 7.30am he steps noisily down the hall, to make enough noise so Mum will hear him and not jump out of her skin as she does almost all the time.

"Good morning Mum!" he says, in his best 'happy to be alive' voice.

"Oh my God!" exclaims Mum, holding on to her heart as though it would jump right out of her chest if her hands weren't there.

"Oh, I'm sorry Mum, I made as much noise as I could," he says, giving her a hug to ease the start she'd just had.

"I didn't know there was anyone here!" she says, amazed that he'd somehow materialised out of nowhere.

"I've been here all night Mum," he replies, hoping she'd put the pieces together.

"Where did you sleep?" she asks, her mind now racing for clues.

"In the back bedroom Mum," he replies, noticing now the root of the confusion.

"What back bedroom? I didn't know there was one," she asks, her mind in a tailspin.

"Here Mum, I'll show you," he says and slowly they make their way up the hall to the back room.

"I didn't know there was a room here," she states, as though this was the very first encounter.

"It used to have a sofa bed here and a cabinet here with a TV on," he says, building a mental picture for her to digest in bite-size pieces.

"I've never been in here before so I wouldn't know," she says, still perplexed by the sudden appearance of a room where there might have been a void.

"We put a single bed in here last April Mum, so we could sleep over," he reminds her, in case any of the evidence sticks.

"Here, in this room?" she asks, seemingly confused by the concept of indoor sleeping.

"Yes, it's too wet outside at night Mum," he says in jest, knowing she'd laugh if she could hear him for even a moment.

"Ha-ha, funny!" she replies, still sharp enough to hear the funny side.

"Here's your room Mum," he moves to point to the light still coming from the room and the little bedside lamp.

"Who left that on?" she asks, claiming diplomatic immunity to all transgressions committed on these premises.

"You were going to sleep in here last night Mum, but must have changed your mind and stopped in the lounge," he suggests, quickly filling in the blanks.

"I don't remember that at all," she says, constantly surprised that recent events keep disappearing from her grasp.

"Would you like some breakfast?" he asks, hoping as she's been up early some sustenance would be welcomed.

They head from the missing bedroom to Mum's bedroom, she opens the curtains, turns off the bedside lamp and watches the big birds on the back lawn eating the bread he'd put out last night.

"What are all those white things on the lawn?" she asks, her glasses still in the lounge possibly contributing to the confusion.

"It's bread for the birds Mum," he says, beginning to wonder where this line of questioning may go.

"Why is it all over the lawn?" she asks, possibly unhappy with the random nature of the bread scattering.

"That's so they all get a piece Mum," he says, still under the delusion that scattering is better than clumping it all in one place.

"It's a bloody mess, that's what it is," she declares, her frown now darkening an otherwise innocent, child-like curiosity.

"Let's get you that breakfast," he says, making a move for the door.

"I can do that," she says, but then no sooner is the statement of intent spoken than the 'dementors' of doubt instantly show up, freezing her to the spot.

He guides her slowly back to the kitchen and proceeds to make the breakfast for one, one slice of toast, one pot of butter, one pot of marmalade, one cup of tea, all done in a jiffy.

He walks her to her favourite chair, helps her assume the comfy position, then returns with the breakfast tray and leaves her to enjoy her toast while he gets his pot of coffee on the go and puts a few dishes away.

A spot of Radio 4, a quick wipe around and tidy up, then he returns to the lounge to sit with his Mum. Her toast eaten, her cup resting firmly on the tray, her head so full of disjointed thoughts she had nodded off under the weight of it all, to rearrange her thoughts perhaps, into some semblance of order.

He looks to the camera, raises his morning coffee and says "cheerio for now" imagining for a moment that a host of folks up there in another realm could hear him and maybe send a glimmer of hope every now and again, as they have been known to do in times such as these.

36. Scattered Pictures...

"Of the smiles we left behind,

Smiles we gave to one another,

For the way we were."

Barbara Streisand echoes off the walls in the space where memories go to rest.

Mum hunts for a pen and something to write on.

"What's our address here where we're staying?" she asks.

"Gloucester Road Mum," I reply and she writes down the full address, then the ages of each of us.

"See that picture of Taid in the kitchen? I want to send it to him where he is now," she continues, picturing him sat somewhere, living and maybe enjoying his breakfast too.

Taid (Welsh for grandfather) died in 1984, the picture she's referring to was taken in 1981 when he was still able to drive from Chester and visit us in Poynton.

Mum finishes the note and files it, along with hundreds, if not thousands, of little pieces of paper in hard to find places. I found some of Mum's old diaries this morning while cleaning, a quick glance showed meticulous accounts from the days before the dementia came.

My brother and I must have left Mum hundreds of notes with our numbers on over the past few years, they disappear as though a cosmic magician is present, spiriting her clues away, keeping us all wondering where they've gone.

In Mum's case, these little notes end up in books as bookmarks, along with tissues, carefully cut kitchen roll and bits of card from old packaging she's saved.

The question about where we are though, reinforces the idea that she's still here on a short break and all the questioning seems to allude to the same idea, how long we're staying, what's on the itinerary today, who's joining us for breakfast etc. So, I play along, pretending too that we're here for a break.

"What's that box on the wall with red dancing, no, walking feet across the front?" Mum asks, pointing vaguely outwards.

"It's an alarm box Mum," I suggest, guessing it's what she's spotted.

"Oh, I've never seen that before," Mum says, reminding me of just how 'in the moment' she is.

The neighbour walks past and heads for the house with the alarm box.

"The lights should change in a moment Mum as the lady goes into her house," I say, hoping this goes to plan.

Mum watches intently as the neighbour enters her front door and turns off her alarm.

"The lights are blue now!" Mum exclaims, amazed by the spectacle.

"She must be in and safe now Mum," I say, hoping Mum's heard.

"Who is?" asks Mum.

"The lady opposite Mum," I reply.

"What lady?" asks Mum.

"The lady who's just gone in and turned off her alarm," I reply.

"Oh yes, I saw her go in," she says, as close to up-to-speed as she can muster.

I'm reminded in this funny moment of just how many times this pattern replays itself each day. Mum spots something, asks a question about it, I answer then Mum's lost what the subject was and we backtrack until she's found it once more.

"Look at that little bird," Mum will say.

"It's a blue tit Mum," I'll reply.

"What is?" Mum will ask and how I long for the days when we'd enjoy watching the world from the caravan window, when we both had our I-Spy eyes on and we'd hear each other's every word and I'd learn to see the magic in what she saw and vice versa.

Such is life, and as is often said these days, 'we are where we are' or 'it is what it is' as though to say 'that's it folks' and 'that's all there is.'

In the comfortable silences, where we sit in the lounge and Mum watches the world like it's her first day on planet Earth, that's where I get to appreciate just how lucky we are.

In her 'swan song', Mum is showing me the priceless beauty of each precious moment. She's showing me her love for life itself.

I'll have to stop there; my eyes are leaking!

37. Any Questions

Mum sits in the conservatory, smiling at the birds on the feeder. Her mind was bursting with questions today from the minute I got in and I really don't know where she gets all her energy from!

We sat together in the lounge and I noticed the pattern replaying. Mum has a fairly limited range of standard questions, generally about four or five main topics, rinsed and repeated infinitum until we break for air, drinks or food.

"What's the name of that house over the road?"

"Why don't they cut that bush down over the road?"

"Does this bird feeder need to come inside?"

"What are those blue lights on that box?"

"What does that number plate say?"

We move to the back of the house to escape the scorching heat of the gas fire. Sat in the conservatory there are four or five different topics, again repeated in double figures until I find a natural break and nip out to bring further refreshments.

"What are those spinner things called?"

"What's that thing on that roof?

"Do those plant pots need painting?"

"Where have all the leaves gone on the trees?"

"What are those birds called?"

I did try to keep count at one point but the number and speed at which the questions came were just too taxing and by 4.30pm I had to cave in and start making dinner. I must have some magnetic type qualities as Mum gave up the comfy seat in the conservatory to come and stand by my side in the kitchen as I made the meal.

The repeated questioning barrage continued in the kitchen and included topics like:

"Why is that wheelie bin outside?"

"Is that your car?"

"Why is that bush still there?"

"What are we having for tea again?"

"Will there be enough for everyone?"

It's a funny thing, this late afternoon and evening meal thing. Mum begins hankering for food, the cooking of the meal, the setting of the table and the serving of the meal... then no sooner has she sat down than her appetite vanishes. It's perhaps to do with the pattern of food making at this time of day, where she clicks into mother mode and remembers the pattern but not necessarily how to recreate it.

The main thing is Mum's been in a good space today, I don't think I got any of the answers wrong and there wasn't a single sign of frustration so that's a good sign!

Lemon cake for M' Ladyship's dessert, so I'd better dash!

38. The Birds are Here!

Mum delights in the little makeshift ramekins on her breakfast tray, one for marmalade, one for butter and one for lemon cheese.

The timing of the toast and the tea, a process of almost military precision. The butler hovering near the toaster, the tray prepared, the kettle boiled and merely waiting for M' Ladyship to emerge from the bedroom, washed, dressed and ready for another unseasonable day in February.

Mum arrives at the kitchen door to brush her hair in the hall mirror.

"Here she is, Queen for a day," I say as Mum brushes her hair and smiles back at me via the mirror.

This is my final cue as the toast pops out of the toaster. Her toast neatly cut in half, I follow Mum with her tray, hoping she doesn't trip over the half-off stocking that's trailing beneath her otherwise neat attire for today.

She sits down, back in the comfy chair she only left half an hour ago. It looked at that point like she may in fact stay there all day in her dressing gown covered by a cosy blanket, but no, she wanted to be dressed for breakfast.

Freshly reinstalled in her chair, I set the tray on her lap and Mum notices the ramekins, still believing this is a guesthouse and remembering having noticed the little pots before.

"Aren't they clever here?" says Mum.

"How's that Mum?" I ask, just to see what she's thinking.

"To not only know what I like, but also to use these little pots!" she says, clearly impressed at exactly the sort of thing she would have done in years gone past.

The road is quiet today. The sky is bright blue. The earlier frost burning off in the morning sunlight. People pass by on their way to the shops or to the railway station. Mum watches each one as though they're the first people she's ever seen.

A tiny blue tit appears on the feeder by her window to Mum's near squeals of delight: "Ooh look, hello little bird!" she says, doubtless wishing the bird could hear her. "Ooh look, its brother has joined her for some food," she says, so happy to see the feeder being used and, like me, delighted to see the birds so close to the window.

One of the birds hops on to the little bush outside the window and bobs around a bit, almost looking in to see Mum before flying off.

This is one of those moments to treasure, one where Mum's free from the anxiety, happy and comfortable in the eternal now.

Long may this moment last.

39. Two Little Boys

"What's the names of those two little boys?" asks Mum as she points at the photos on the fireplace of my brother and myself in 1966.

"That's Robin and Martin," I reply, wondering where this will go.

"Are they still called that today?" asks Mum, her mind scrambled with disjointed thoughts and umpteen unfathomable questions.

"Yes, I'm Martin and Robin was here this weekend," I reply, pointing at myself as Mum is still preferring not to use her hearing aids.

"You're not Martin are you?" she asks, giving me a full scan and her best eye-straining focus.

"Yes Mum I am," I reply.

"How long have you been Martin?" Mum asks and my mind whirs as I think up a suitable response.

"Since I was born I think?" I ask, just in case the answer's wrong.

"I didn't know that," Mum says, a confused or befuddled look on her face.

It's one of those oft-repeated questions where the usual response to my honest answer is "Never in a million years are you Martin!" or "Never, never, never!" which usually comes with the threat of violence, so I always answer with caution just in case. What's that they say, 'Expect the best, prepare for the worst'?

I change the subject before she gets even more confused...

"Have you seen any birds on the feeder today?" I ask, pointing out of the window.

Mum looks at me, then out of the window, then back at me again.

Her face reveals a question but without the words.

"Have there been any birds on the feeder?" I try once more with slightly different words.

"Oh, birds on the feeder!" she replies, finally putting the words together into a proper question.

"Have you seen any?" I ask again.

"Have I seen any what?" Mum replies.

"Birds?" I ask, noticing the difficulty she's having.

"Birds?" asks Mum, wondering perhaps why I'd be asking such a daft question.

"Yes, birds on the feeder?" I try.

"What about them?" Mum asks, still looking perplexed.

"Have you seen any birds eating seeds from the feeder?" I try once more.

"Huh?" asks Mum, her concentration broken by another passing thought.

"Another cup of tea Mum?" I ask just to test if it's my volume and clarity or Mum's hearing.

"Ooh, I'll say!" she replies, sharp as a tack and quick as a flash.

And so it came to pass that the son realised that today might be one for sitting in silence while gazing out of the window and letting his Mum ask the questions.

I make Mum another cup of tea and return to sit with her in the lounge. I sit in Dad's old chair and fiddle with the camera while Mum smiles at the passing clouds. Within moments she's drifting off to sleep. Her head tilts downwards until her chin is nearly on her chest. It can't possibly be comfy, but it's exactly how her father used to nap.

Then she awakes, immediately looks at me and says, "I must get changed for church later but I haven't got a hat."

"That's OK Mum, it's Monday today so church is next Sunday," I reply.

"Oh, thank goodness," she says, a wave of relief washing over her.

Over the course of the weekend Mum's managed to consume an entire double packet of custard creams somewhere in between the relief carers and my brother's visits. I only know this because I make sure she's always stocked up as I also serve biscuits to help with the taking of her tablets.

Right now Mum is engrossed in a Pam Ayres book from 1976 and loving every page. She's got sandwiches on a plate and little slice of cake, another cup of tea and the fire on full blast. The window cleaner has literally just been but the memory of his being there has gone from her mind already.

One of this week's little projects, to keep Mum using her brain, is pickled onions.

I've got some jars soaking in a bowl of water so I can get the labels off. Mum's recipe is ready to be called upon as an aide-memoire for her. Fingers crossed, these will taste just like they did every time Mum made them in the good old days before we all got so busy with life and had to buy everything instead of making it ourselves.

With a little luck I'll get some good pictures of Mum and the pickling process.

If I could turn back time I'd head back to 1970 and capture all these precious moments on film, you know, the ones where Mums weave their magic in the background of our lives and everything is held together by something but you're too young to know exactly what it is?

Better dash, things to do and jars to prepare!

40. Eggshells

Neither a child nor an adult would get away with bad behaviour in public, but in Mum's case, the only solution appears to be kindness.

Given that her body is getting increasingly sensitive, too sore for the carers to apply skin cream, too painful to have her nails cut, it struck me today how even her sensibilities have also become like open wounds.

Gary came today, my dear friend from art college days. He came bringing a beautiful arrangement of flowers from himself and

Annette. Mum was delighted as she often is on the rare occasions a dashing young visitor arrives, then she drifts off, unable to hear normal conversation, unable to make small talk, she disappears in her mind and watches the clouds out of the window.

Then my partner Carol arrived. The house was suddenly buzzing and for some reason Mum thinks I'm my father again and immediately sees Carol as a threat, even though she's loved her as a daughter for 20 years. She sits there giving me the evil eye, watching me like a hawk watches its prey.

Gary has to leave and once we've waved our goodbyes from the window and I wish we'd had longer to catch up, the lounge turns into a scene from *Gunfight at the OK Corral*.

I'm unwisely sat in Dad's old chair, Carol's in the guest chair and Mum's in her favourite chair, toying with the metaphorical holster by her side.

Tumbleweed blows through the space between us, Mum's eyes go all squinty like Lee Van Cleef as she weighs up her options. She can't hear us, even when we try to include her in the conversation, it's as though our words are in Mongolian, a language Mum never really took to for some reason.

She stares out of the window, then stares at Carol and me, then at the clouds once more as she tries to imagine what's going on. I'd already made lunch earlier and left it ready in the kitchen to bring out when Mum was hungry. The hunger didn't really come, although it did get mentioned when her sandwich was delivered and she said she wasn't hungry.

Mum decides to head off to the conservatory, though at this point we just thought she'd gone to her bedroom to get changed, as she often does. Twenty minutes later she hasn't returned so we go to check on her. She's sitting in the conservatory reading a book and nursing a cold cup of tea.

"We haven't had any lunch yet," Mum declares as we enter the conservatory.

"We had some earlier Mum but you weren't hungry," I remind her.

"Oh, don't you worry about me will you?" she snaps, her fine white hair about to ignite.

"I'll bring yours now if you're ready," I say, and head to the kitchen to get Mum's plate.

"What's this?" she says, as I hand her the lovingly made salmon and cucumber in a bread roll under a cling film cover.

"I don't want this!" she exclaims and makes a move to fling the plate across the conservatory.

Luckily, I used to be a goalkeeper so I catch the plate and bring it to a safe stop on the pouffe.

"Would you like some beans on toast Mum?" I ask, like a patient saint, in case it's just the cold sandwich she's not keen on.

"Oh, don't worry about me, I'd rather starve!" she says, reminding me of a stroppy teenager in a TV soap opera.

"How about some nice soup Mum?" I venture, hoping this may be the answer.

"Ooh, that sounds nice," she says, her mood lifting off her like a strong breeze shifts a low-lying cloud sometimes.

I head off to whip up a quick soup on a tray with some crusty bread. I return in a flash and deliver Mum's soup, she seems to be delighted, though I've seen enough eggshells scattered around to know when to tread lightly.

Not long after, it's time for Carol to leave so Mum heads back after her soup to the lounge. She asks where Carol is heading. "Yorkshire," Carol replies, and quick as a flash Mum puts two and two together and gets five.

"That's why Fred keeps going to Yorkshire is it?"

Before we knew it, Mum had fired her first bullets. Carol was wounded but not fatally, I was hit but it was only a flesh wound.

The last time Carol came, she and I got the same treatment. Carol was suddenly the floozy and I was my Dad. All the lovely times we'd spent together over the years tarnished now by the effect the dementia has had on Mum's mind.

We say our goodbyes in the hallway. Carol heads off. Mum and I wave from the window. My heart is pounding and the butterflies have come out for a flutter too.

Mum stays in her chair to wave, simmering though like a pressure cooker.

Rationally, you could say that this is clearly just a simple case of mistaken identity. However, one of the symptoms of dementia is that the sufferer thinks that everyone else is ill and not them. In this case we're reminded that whilst Mum's short-term memory is shot to pieces, what she can recall from the past year is very selective and quite often completely unfiltered in its sharing.

Carol and I used to come and do Mum and Dad's garden for years. The last time Carol came Mum shooed her off and whilst she understands the effects of the dementia, it doesn't make it any easier to accept when a loved one sees you suddenly through a new and quite faulty lens.

As I've eluded to in earlier missives, 'all we can do is all we can do' and whilst in the heat of any feisty moment our human instinct is to challenge certain behaviours, in this case all we can do is imagine the floor coated in eggshells and our role now is to merely tread lightly upon them, as Mum would have done had she been in our shoes.

Ah well, we can but try!

41. Still Going Strong

The carer left in a scurry, with Mum rudely shooing her out of the door while waving her walking stick at her. There's not much one can say in such moments other than pass an acknowledging smile of understanding to the victim.

The admonishments continue, only now directed at me, which I guess is fair enough, I'm breathing therefore I'm a good enough target for now. I connect myself up to the reserve tank of loving kindness and offer some new distractions to ease the turmoil in Mum's head, the Pam Ayres book comes to the rescue!

I'm reminded of the imaginary scene of someone comforting a lioness with a thorn in her paw. It's a dangerous task either way. I wonder how the historical Daniel would have handled this.

Mum settles for a while. I recuperate for a while. The Earth continues to speed around the sun at 66,660 miles per hour, although it seems way slower than that when we're in any kind of tussle over funerals or missing relatives. Still, it's all in the eyes of the official perceiver I suppose.

A few snacks and drinks for Mum later, including the all-important bedtime cup of 'hot chocolate drinking chocolate' and it's heading rapidly past my bedtime and into the 'past-myself' zone.

In the space of the time it takes to say 'Jack Robinson', Mum has somehow emptied her handbag and neatly arranged the contents on to her chair. I'm impressed by the neatness of the arrangements, it's just like photographers do when they say "And here's what's in my bag!"

"What are you looking for Mum?" I ask, in case it's something I may be able to find elsewhere.

"I'm trying to find…" starts Mum and we're left suspended once more in weightlessness, like spacemen floating in wonderment high above the Earth.

I remain silent, conscious that guessing or adding my guesses to the equation only makes it harder for her.

"It's not in here," she says, turning the now empty bag upside down.

"How about the side pocket?" I say, noticing it's still zipped shut.

"Nope, it's not in there either," says Mum, her hand rummaging around in the side pocket.

"That's a nice collection of scissors Mum," I say, remembering the scissor incident last year and wondering if these are the miniature versions, like pocket handguns for self-defence.

"Yes, I don't know where they've all come from," declares Mum as though she's stood with the douanier at a French airport.

I check if it's OK to turn the fire down as it's bedtime now. Mum's ready, by the look of things, so I turn down the fire and head to Mum's room to turn on her bedside light.

By 11.00pm and bearing in mind she's been up since 4.00am, she's still full of beans and causing mischief. We say our 'night-nights' and I close my door.

Knock, knock. Mum wants to say goodnight to her parents who must still be in the conservatory. I turn on the lights for her to see for herself. Further confusion ensues. I diffuse the situation somehow. I slowly and patiently usher her towards her room, say 'night-night' number two.

Knock, knock.

"How do we turn these lights off?" Mum asks, pondering on the lights in the lounge she's turned off thousands of times over the years.

I head to the lounge and turn off all the lights with Mum doing her best to stand in the way.

'Night-night' number three over as though it was the first.

Door closed, deep breath. Silence.

Knock, knock.

"Should I wait up for Dad?" asks Mum, genuinely concerned for his absence.

"I'll keep an ear out for him Mum," I say, only by way of an assurance.

"Oh, all right then if you're sure," she says.

"Night-night," she says and we hug for the fourth time as though it was the first.

Door closed, thoughts of how this must be it now.

Knock, knock.

"We've had a note through the door to say about leaving the hall light on," says Mum

"Yes, that's right Mum," I say, and assure her this is the norm, too tired now to do the 'leaving the landing light on' joke.

"Night-night," we say and time for me to sit in the dark to recapture the stillness within.

I hear Mum pad off to bed, then return to use the bathroom, then pad back to bed after a brief pace up and down the hall.

It's now Thursday. I'm up at the usual time. Mum's still a' bed. I wonder if that was her moving around last night and did she go to bed assured or worried? Hopefully assured I assure myself, assuredly.

An hour later, I was going to say 'than usual' but there is no usual about any of this, I hear Mum open her bedroom curtains. Butler duties attended to, another cup of tea is made ready and waiting by her chair. The fire is on and the curtains are opened, the breakfast tray's awaiting toast but otherwise ready in the kitchen. I usher Mum to the lounge for our morning observations through the 'rainy window'.

If you looked, even with a fine toothcomb, you'd never imagine what went on yesterday. The comings and goings, the joy of visitors, the ups and downs, the stick waving and bag emptying. All you'd see was a lady fast approaching her 92nd birthday looking as happy as happy can be. And that dear friends is all we could ever ask for.

Must dash.

42. Domestic Duties

There's never a dull day, even when it's a dull day. There's always something to do and tidy and fix and prepare and wash. One of today's chores was card writing, something Mum used to take great delight in, the choosing, the buying, the embellishing, the writing, the pouring of emotions into the celebration of a special day.

Nowadays she still enjoys the writing part, though the context or memory of whom it's for rarely lasts the time it takes to write out the well wishes within.

I've taken to using the slow cooker for a number of the week's meals, so the house is often full of cooking smells. The washing machine spins away in the background, the front door gets opened and closed, each time letting in gusts of cool yet getting warmer spring air.

There have been a few more spillages of late, it's my fault for saying Mum never spills a drop, I must have tempted fate a little too much that day. What's interesting though, from a butler's point of view, is how it's never, ever, ever M' Ladyship that spills anything, even though there's only the two of us here.

I managed to wash and dry about six of Mum's jumpers yesterday, quite a triumph on the logistics front, as if caught carrying said items, one is always reprimanded for daring to do such things.

The thing is, we're heading rapidly towards the kinds of days where I could take Mum out for day trips and given how she always took pride in her appearance, the food stains on her clothes suggest I'm not doing a good job of caring for her, well they do to me anyway.

Talking of getting caught, Mum caught me making a meal the other day, I was busy preparing the vegetables and chopping onions when Mum walked in and asked, "What are you doing?"

"I'm making a meal for later Mum," I replied nervously.

"Oh, don't you be doing things like that, I'll do the cooking," she says, forgetting how she threw in the towel on the cooking front while Dad was still alive.

I somehow managed to divert Mum towards the kettle and went with her to the lounge to drink said drink while plotting my escape back to the kitchen.

It's a sensitive thing this pride business, especially with someone who's been the chief cook and bottle washer for so long but also doesn't realise that most days she can't find anything in the kitchen let alone cook with it.

Mum's busy right now with an old notepad of hers from the 1980s. It's full of all kinds of notes in both shorthand and cursive form.

I took Mum a drink earlier, her chin was on her chest, she heard me approach, lifted her head, opened her eyes and said, "We need to take the things with us when we go."

"You were dreaming Mum," I say, sitting down beside her.

"Oh that's a relief," she says, genuinely glad there's someone there to remind her.

And therein lies the challenge Mum faces so often, what's a dream and what's real. Mind you, there's many a day when I'm right there with her on that one!

Right, better be off, the dryer's finished and thanks to all the cutbacks, it's all down to the butler now to fold the laundry.

43. Skip to My Loo

Well, it's supposed to be 'to my Lou' and there's definitely been no skipping here today, but nevertheless we sang it and other songs to lighten the moment as we made our way gingerly from the lounge to the bathroom.

In fact, it took us a few minutes just to get from Mum's favourite chair to the next chair, literally only a few steps, but Mum's legs and feet won't work today and each step has been like her very first ones as a toddler.

We got as far as the next chair with me holding her upright as best I could, then I saw the walker in the hallway and asked if this would be a better way. Mum agreed, so holding herself up against the second chair while attempting to cross her legs, I made a swift move for the walker.

This was a much better way and gave Mum a little more independence in getting to the loo under her own steam. When you're feeling as weak as Mum, little things like this must make a difference to the overall sense of conquering the body's unwillingness to cooperate.

A few minutes later and we've made it. A simple bathroom break, something we all take for granted, suddenly feels like *Challenge Anneka!*

I hear the loo flush and head back with a freshly laundered and lavender-fresh smelling dressing gown, warm from being near a radiator and a welcome contrast to the old one that I managed to wrestle off her before she went in.

The day has been one of rest. This follows a fairly normal night where Mum only got up for one wander around at 3.00am. Otherwise, the butler has been on call all day, even leaving Mum with a handbell to ring if she needed anything.

Using a combination of intuition and son's love I managed to arrive with food, drinks and tissues before she even had a chance to use the aforementioned handbell. Ironically, when there was an actual emergency, the one where we needed to 'Skip to my Loo', Mum had forgotten about the bell and was instead whispering "help" at the top of her whisper. Luckily I heard her after the second call.

On a very sad note, our dear friend Andy passed away this morning. Mum being in hospital with a chest infection for a couple of days gave me the time to see him a last time this week. It's amazing how these things can work out sometimes.

Andy and his wife Joyce have been regular readers of Mum's adventures and enjoyed hearing some of them read out when we got together over recent months. I'd always tell Mum about Andy's adventures too and whilst she never met him, she knew all about his double lung transplant as this was in 2013, the same year Mum got her dementia diagnosis, and of Andy playing the flugelhorn in a brass band.

Mum has looked so weak since she got home, each time I've gone into her room she'd be asleep and barely breathing. Luckily she's woken when I've made just the right amount of noise as I move quietly around with food and drinks. I guess it's all part of the butler role, to be seen as required but rarely otherwise heard.

Another marked change has been how Mum has welcomed me with open arms each time I've arrived with something, almost as though it's her first time of seeing me in how many years?

The relief carer is arriving any minute, so I'll be leaving you now.

44. Help!

I'm not sure whether it's a dream or where the heck I am. I've slept in three different beds in the space of a week. It's 1.45am, I've been fast asleep since 11.00pm and Mum was safely tucked up in the lounge at 10.00pm.

Now the sudden sounds of movement whisk me out of wherever I thought I was sleeping to Mum's nocturnal world of fumbles, bumps and flumps. This is the third night in a row that sleep's been broken in the wee small hours.

Mum's been very unsteady on her feet since coming home from hospital. The old familiar sounds of shuffling feet or the oft-heard flump of the slippers replaced now with a new auditory combination that goes scuff-shuffle-flump, scuff-shuffle-flump.

The evening routine, if you can call it that, is fairly well practised now and Mum appears to be nicely calm and settled when I tuck her in for the night with her hot chocolate. The part we can't seem to tame is the night confusion, where she'll get up to go to the loo then struggle with where she is and how she got there.

The usual but still unexpected cacophony of noise is what awakes me, the initial fumbling with the lounge door, then the flicking off and on of lights, the torrential flush of the loo, the creaking of the floorboards as Mum reads the sign on my door to let her know I'm in here. I lie there and night-dream of ear muffs and black-out curtains.

Mum opens and closes the front door. The darkness of the outside possibly affirming the lateness or rather the earliness of the hour. More light switching as she checks the clocks all tell the same unwelcome story. Then the tuneful chiming of the wind chimes by the door as she bumps into them, once tentatively, then a second time with more gusto.

As the last of the chimes finishes its chiming, I hear Mum heading back to the lounge with a scuff-shuffle-flump. Then silence. It's now 2.15am. The bags under my eyes must resemble those of a late-night BBC news reader from the 1970s.

Aside from an almost feisty moment when a relief carer called yesterday before lunch, Mum's been, for want of a better description, quite sedate. The chesty cough has remained and she doesn't have the strength to clear it, so the rattle turns nearly to a choking situation that in turn leads to sneezing fits.

I'm glad to report that she's still eating well though and M' Ladyship's still had no issue with the cook's cooking, so all is well at least on that front.

In this past year of caring for Mum, I've never seen her sleep as much as this past few days. The thought of days out seems some way off at this point, even getting her into a wheelchair looks like it could be a challenge in itself as Mum's strength looks to have been all used up sparring with the ninja nurses earlier this week.

The other noticeable change is the frequency of Mum's calls of "Help!" I got five calls in the space of 15 minutes last night after our meal. Each time it was something I couldn't help with at all, like coughing, but the mere presence of someone can help sometimes and that's what seemed to be the case.

In my imagined picture of what the house would be like while caring for Mum it's filled with music, or plays on the radio or we're sitting watching TV documentaries like she used to. The reality is quite different. The sound of music is reserved for the rare moments when Mum's in the mood, the radio has to be on at almost inaudible levels so as not to disturb the silence and the TV is simply never on these days.

The plus point to the silence in the house, aside from its meditative qualities, narrows down to one thing: at least I can hear Mum when she shouts "Help!" and be there in a jiffy.

Ah well, it's time to see if I can remove Mum's breakfast tray without disturbing her. Wish me luck!

45. The Counting of Blessings

She sleeps and sleeps. The faintest sound of breathing is all I can hear. She was up at 4.45am from the lounge then away to her bed.

I've heard it suggested that having things orderly and consistent can be a coping mechanism, so be it, orderly it is.

'Mr Dependable' the butler arrives at M' Ladyship's room with her first cup of tea. M' Ladyship is still asleep. He tries again an hour later, just the sound of gentle breathing could be heard. Perhaps some everyday noises may stir her into action if for nothing else than curiosity.

The plastic clattering sounds of coat hangers being gathered up and put into carrier bags. The sound of the washing machine going on and the hunt for her other dressing gown to accompany it for a spin. The clinking of plates and glass being put away from last night. The footsteps up and down the hall.

Then, just as in a scene from a *Tom and Jerry* cartoon, where Tom gets a fright and his body turns like an X-ray scan as his skeleton departs from his body, Mum appears from nowhere and asks, "Is there anybody in there?" while pointing at the bathroom.

I feel that cold tingly shudder of fright as it passes like an electric charge from top to toe and back up again. It's not that Mum's in any way frightening, aside from when she's got her red jumper on, it's simply that literally a minute earlier she was fast asleep and tucked up in her bed!

Delighted though I was to see her actually up, this 10.30am arrival was unexpected and still worth the jolt. In truth I'd have taken a bullet for this moment.

Mum being up, I set about making some more noise and get to work with the vacuum cleaner, in here, over there, up there too, 'run for cover,' shouted the thin-as-a-wisp like spiders in the corners.

I pottered like this for another hour, Mum kept popping out of her room to ask for assistance. I laid out clothes for today on her bed, made sure she had underwear, a vest, stockings, trousers, a jumper, a cardigan and even nice matching navy blue shoes.

I can feel a tear or three welling up as I think about describing how good it is to see her up and dressed after what looked very much like she was going to take to her bed for the long haul. I count my blessings instead, remembering the scientific fact that no two things can exist in the same place and time.

Mum is now reinstalled in the lounge, the getting there a challenge in itself. Tablets and biscuits on a tiny plate, late breakfast on a tray. Hair brushed, shawl on, glasses sparkling and a fresh cuppa ready when she is.

I snap a quick portrait to capture this absolutely priceless moment and go to grab the laptop so I can jot these observations down at the dining table. Mum starts her own observations while looking out of the window at the view she's recorded mentally for 20 plus years…

"Those tulips are bursting with unexpected colour."

"Did you move all the cards off the windowsill?"

"The lady over the road is mowing her lawn again. She does it every morning now first thing."

"It looks like it could be a nice day!"

Meanwhile, the dryer tumbles away in the background. The birds feed from the feeder. Clouds make their way from here to there. Children off school walk or ride past. The fire roars on a slightly lower setting. The opened window lets in tiny blasts of fresh spring air. Life goes on and I'll need a bloody big calculator to count my blessings today.

Got to dash, eyes leaking for some reason!

46. Here Comes the Mum

It appears that there's a very fine line between entropy and recharging the old batteries. In Mum's case, she's found the long rest to be restorative and before long she'd resumed full-on questioning duties which lasted until the evening carer arrived at 7.30pm.

It's quite miraculous to see Mum go from what appears to be a state of almost on the bridge between this life and the next, then to see her on her feet once more. Mind you, it is nearly Easter!

Her resurgence began around mid-afternoon yesterday, very unsteady on her feet and glad of the walking stick or something to hold her upright, but none the less, determined to explore the 'holiday home'.

I say 'holiday home' – it's Mum's house and has been since 1998 or so, but as mentioned in previous updates, to Mum every day feels like a holiday in a strangely if not vaguely familiar guesthouse, somewhere near the coast.

Mum followed me around the rest of the afternoon as I brought in washing from the line in the garden or folded other clothes already dried from the previous night's mischief (mischief being something someone else has done, like spilling hot chocolate on a certain blanket while someone else wasn't looking!).

It happened again overnight, 'someone' had spilt hot chocolate on her blanket while she was asleep. "Who can it be?" he says in a grown-up, parental type voice. I'm then of course reminded of all the thousands of times Mum washed my clothes when I was younger and also I've now got an experiential understanding of why she was always in the kitchen, literally chained to the sink or the cooker.

Yes, it can be tough when you're backed into a corner and getting the third degree on an unanswerable subject; however, these are such precious times and as we all know, there has to be a 'down' in order for there to be an 'up'.

Mum is just about to begin a 'follow Martin around the house with a bowl of fruit salad' game. At this point though she's playing with the blinds to move the sunlight around the kitchen and off the fruit salad I'd just put in the sun to gently warm up some of the fruit that had been in the fridge.

The fruit salad got some unexpected food miles on it, going from the kitchen to the lounge, back to the kitchen, then to the conservatory, then back to the kitchen, then the lounge again. Each trip being a risky one as Mum is struggling to keep herself upright let alone a heavy glass bowl.

I've learned not to step in and rescue her in these kinds of situations, merely to stand close by, trying to look unconcerned, ready to catch her or to aid her with whatever she decides is too much and see if I could help her with it. It's the same with walking to the loo or wherever; the walker or a stick is preferable as it affirms her own abilities.

An hour or so after we'd had our dinner, Mum was finding her second hunger and asking if I wanted anything to eat every few minutes. At one juncture, Mum went for more cutlery from the kitchen drawer.

"We've had our dinner Mum," I said, for the 12th time, this time though just to selfishly avoid the whole table setting routine as I'd already been on my feet for 12 hours.

This led to a "Whatever you say, you're the boss!" response and it was clear that the old battery was working fine once more!

Today the signs are looking good. She's had a few naps this morning since I did the dawn patrol, now she's breakfasted, enjoyed a couple of sips of tea and is up and about for an explore.

On that note, I'd better get her tablets and a biscuit ready!

47. All the Right Notes

You've probably heard the old comedy line about playing all the right notes, just not in the right order? That pretty much summed up Mum's day today.

She's back up and about after a week or so of long rests and plenty of sleep. Now she's dressed, up with the larks and generally enjoying her newly rediscovered mobility around the house.

"Where are the stairs in this place?" Mum asks on one of her missions.

"We're in a bungalow today Mum, which room are you looking for?" I ask.

"I want to get upstairs to my room," she says, still looking curiously into the bathroom for clues.

"Have you lost something Mum?" I ask, in case I could help her find it.

"Yes, all my clothes, I want to get dressed!" she replies, unaware that she's already fully dressed.

I guide Mum to her bedroom, open the wardrobe doors and help her pick out the next set of clothes she'd rather be wearing. New trousers, a different jumper, then a frenetic search for a matching pair of shoes, then a missing jewellery box she remembers from way back when.

Newly togged up, Mum heads to the kitchen to make another cup of tea to go with the one that's already waiting for her by her chair. All along I'm encouraging her to do the things she always used to do and see if this helps her join up the dots in this unfathomable equation.

Mum's washed the dishes twice today, the second time resulting in a wet sleeve on her jumper, this in turn led to costume change number three for today. This entailed a new jumper again plus a different necklace, the previous one being the wrong colour, stupid.

We managed a sit down and a good hour of garden observations this afternoon, Mum even suggesting she will get the ladders out as her next job so she can start trimming the ivy off the neighbour's garage roof. Definitely a case of the mind being the most willing participant in this venture, luckily it stayed in the 'good ideas' file.

Another idea that occurred to M' Ladyship as she checked around the estate was the emptying and replanting of all the planters near the wall. A job I did last summer and one Mum would have loved in her younger years. Who knows, maybe this year we'll get her outside planting pots at some point!

I read to Mum in the late afternoon, she watched me, enthralled like a child listening to her favourite story. The tale was about my friend Andy whose funeral was yesterday and Mum kept asking if he'd died, who he was, where was he from and so on, but otherwise enjoying the description of the day.

By teatime Mum was into everything like a three-year-old, cutlery from the kitchen drawers, plates from the cupboards, up and down the hall, into each room in turn looking for missing relatives, fretting in each room as everyone had gone out without telling her and worrying about the grown-up children and their whereabouts now their tea is ready.

It was said last week that I might be risking 'killing Mum with kindness'. I laughed inside at the irony of such a thing as a son actually somehow reversing the world's oldest and still currently trending qualities of a mother's love. All feedback is useful, so my takeaway was the idea that maybe I should try doing less and risking the consequences anyway, you know, those unimaginable consequences that can only be foreseen if you're on the regular receiving end of them.

We ate our meal together, surrounded by additional plates and cutlery. I made Mum a dessert of peaches and cream, then headed to the back to phone home. Since then, roughly an hour and half ago, Mum has been continuously wandering the rooms again looking for her missing family.

The relief carer's visit interrupted the pattern but not exactly in a welcome way, she was barely through the door before Mum started on her. 'Ah well, we can't have it all ways' I thought to myself. There's no 'off switch' with dementia, we get the symptoms we get and that's pretty much the way it is.

Underneath all this though, Mum's still in there so, as they say in Shakespeare's *Henry V, Act III*... "Once more unto the breach, dear friends, once more..."

Until next time!

48. School's Out

"I can't go to school today," says Mum with a very sorry looking and regretful expression on her just woken face.

"That's OK Mum," I say to reassure her in the moment.

I'd found her fast asleep in Dad's chair earlier, hardly a sign of breathing to be seen, just the peaceful stillness of deep sleep. She heard me in the kitchen and got up for a wander before heading this time to her comfy chair where the strain begins to show.

Her eyelids weigh heavily upon her desire to look out of the window and sleep wins the battle of wills, for a short while at least. I make a tiny noise as I put my cup down on the table beside me, and Mum, who can't hear a word that's said under normal circumstances, awakes for a moment to see what's moved.

"It looks like being a nice day," she manages before the eyelids fall once more.

Her head bows down slowly as though being let down gently by an unseen hand.

A car goes past and her eyes open once more.

"Are they all going to school?" Mum asks, as the 8.30am fashion parade passes her window.

"They are Mum," I say, avoiding too long a reply in case it makes her work too hard to hear it.

Her eyes close once more, the arms of Morpheus pull her from this plain to the other and she's off flying once more, drifting between thoughts and nothingness.

"Where's Daddy?" she says, her eyes still closed.

I leave the silence to work its magic and the thought leaves her as quickly as it arrived.

Mum slept in Dad's old chair last night, wrapped warmly in her cosy blanket, cheese and crackers to one side, hot chocolate to the other, a book on her lap and a lamp to read by and the fire set to a safer level.

It was a peaceful end to an otherwise frenetic day filled with confusion and mentally exhausting activity.

Mum's exercise needs were met yesterday by the continual need to find missing relatives. Up and down, up and down, in and out of rooms, checking and double-checking as though long passed relatives were playing an undiscoverable game of hide and seek with her.

The worries about dinner began at 3.00pm and didn't let up until we were sat down and actually eating at 5.00pm. As it transpired she wasn't really hungry, merely playing out a lifetime's routine.

"These potatoes are cold," she complained. I quickly rushed her plate into the kitchen for a warm.

"These potatoes are too hot," she continued.

"You're supposed to blow on them," I reminded her.

"I can't eat anything, I'm not hungry," she replied and there ended two hours of questioning, worrying, checking on numbers, imagining scenarios and gathering of cutlery.

Mum retired to her comfy chair and I set about washing up. I let Mum help with the putting away as she had another quick burst of helpful energy. Clean cups in the microwave, dishes in the bin cupboard, glasses on the china cups rack, knives in the wooden spoons holder…

I watched as she looked for what she thought were the right places and left her to decide where things went. 'I'll move them later,' I thought, as right now she's happy doing the 'putting away'. The busyness though took its toll and Mum was worn out again, needing to sit down after all the steps she'd done earlier in the day going back and forth, forth and back.

Thankfully, an old copy of a Bill Bryson book caught her attention and she kept hold of it for the rest of the evening. Each time I came bearing gifts of tea or snacks to make up for the lack of a main meal, Mum was engrossed in Bill's writing and only looked up briefly to say "thanks".

By 10.45pm I was flagging so brought Mum the customary evening mug of hot chocolate. By the morning, she'd eaten the crackers, drunk the hot chocolate and snacked on the fruit I'd left. Dementia can rob the sensation of hunger, but it does no harm to leave things to hand just in case!

Anyway, let's see what today brings, meanwhile it's time for some butlering.

49. All Things Must Pass

"When I think of it, I wouldn't like to live on my own... I'd be frightened!" says Mum, as she watches the lady across the road tending to her chores. And there, in summary M'lud, is the dilemma before the court today... how to keep M' Ladyship in the manner to which she has become accustomed.

A large elephant enters the room and stands between Mum, myself and the view out on to the front garden. The elephant is carrying a beautifully embroidered banner declaring that 'all things must pass' and sadly its message rings true.

Whilst Mum and Dad worked and saved all their lives to provide for such times, the funds are diminishing quickly and so much so we'll probably have to sell up here and look at Mum going into a home by autumn. These precious tumultuous days are unfortunately numbered.

Mum and I continue with our daily observations, the elephant sits down by the fire, his trunk heading probingly towards Mum's freshly filled bowl of Everton mints and smiles at me knowingly, the way only elephants can do.

"That little chicken is a chicken now," starts Mum, as she watches the solar-powered dancing daisy bobbing from left to right and back as it does every day in anything resembling sunlight.

"I wonder if they'll do something with that yellow bush over the road?" she continues, as though it should be possible to redesign neighbours' gardens for them.

"It's not a very nice day!" she declares, thankfully unaware of the elephant sat with us and happy to be on the inside looking out.

Meanwhile the hearing aids chirp away to each other as they do whenever they're left together. The church bells climb in again through the partly opened window. The clocks tick-tock and the fire roars, all amplified as future memories to be savoured now even more thanks to the elephant's presence.

The four suet balls in the bird feeder that looked for ages as though they wouldn't get eaten are now down to three nearly gone remnants. A jackdaw positions himself precariously on the feeder and pecks away at the balls until a wood pigeon comes to join the party. Mum's transfixed at the spectacle, almost as though these are the first birds she's ever seen and such is the gift of this illness, the ability to see things through the eyes of an infant.

Piles of books gather neatly on tables and beside the sofa, history books of Liverpool and Chester, a colouring book and felt pens for rainy days, magazines piled up ready to go into temporary hiding again and her current read, Bill Bryson, lies close to hand on the sofa. I head into the kitchen to get Mum another cup of tea, now that she's finished her cornflakes. In the washing-up bowl awaits the cups and plates from last night's supper frenzy.

At 9.00pm last night Mum decided she was hungry, I offered to get her something but she wanted to get it herself, as she's 'been looking after herself for years' apparently!

I stood in the hallway and listened, close enough to step in if required. The biscuit tin rattled, then another biscuit tin rattled, the crinkling of wrappers, the closing of the lids. This rattling and fumbling continued for a good 15 minutes. I moved to a seat down the hall. The kettle boiled, and then it got refilled and boiled again, then again. Forty-five minutes later it all went quiet, so I went to inspect the scene.

Mum was sat in the lounge, triumphant, with a tray. On the tray were two cups of tea with milk, some crackers and a biscuit. In the kitchen half a dozen biscuits lay on the top beside the tin, next to the kettle, two cups filled with tea and milk. In the microwave, another cup filled with warmed-through milk.

Sat here this morning, taking in the wholeness of the scene, I hear my father's voice as he sides with the elephant and says, "And so we say farewell to this wonderful panorama" and long lists of practical things that need attending to cascade before me like ticker-tape streamers on the fourth of July.

The elephant is right, 'all things must pass' for now though at least, as Mum sips on another cup of tea and all is right with the world. I wish I could summon up a pot of gold under that metaphorical rainbow and save Mum from having to leave this place she loved before the illness took hold.

Duties call and the show must go on, so I'll have to say with a heavy heart 'cheerio' for now.

50. The Days Between

Mum sleeps, then awakes, then drifts some more.

In the garden we're in the days between the ending of the rowan tree blossom that sits like cauliflower florets all over the once small sapling and the beginning of the honeysuckle that's bursting its way through the beech hedge.

It's one of those days for chores, where Mum's content to sit and watch from the comfort of her favourite chair, lifting her legs up, like we used to do as children as the vacuum cleaner comes around.

A procession of cups of freshly made tea followed her usual breakfast of cornflakes. She'd got up from her bed this morning at dawn, opened all the curtains and wrapped herself in the cosy blanket before settling into the pilot's seat of her well-tuned time machine.

New suet balls in the bird feeder this morning meant that there were at least some little birds to add to the view.

"Oooh, hello!" she says, as a blue tit lands on to the feeder for a quick nibble at the suet balls.

"Go and tell your friends now," she says, excitedly, as it flies away seconds later.

I prepare a simple lunch and bring it to her on a tray right on the strike of 12.00, the church bells of St George's affirming the 'ship-shape and Bristol fashion' feel of the house today after all the chores.

Mum's nodded off again and doesn't even hear me bring her tray. I set it down beside her and eat my lunch at the table. Seeing her like this, drifting between two worlds, I wonder again if our shared dream will be realised, the dream of her finding the pearly gates, here at home, peacefully in her sleep, safe in the knowledge we're here for her.

Meanwhile, in the background, my brother and I are hoping for the best and planning for the worst. The worst being the money running out and her dying alone in a strange place and without us at her side.

I've grown to love these days between. The unpredictability, the ups and downs, the peace that exists between the flurries of frenetic activity. I wish Dad was still around to enjoy the new regime and us taking the strain.

Anyhow, I'd better go and check once more, to see if Mum's awake and ready for lunch or still flying her time machine somewhere high over Lyme Cage, the old stone tower on the hillside I used to see with her from my bedroom window at number 8 Queensway in the early 1960s.

Who knows, she may be flying over Bootle or Chester or Crosby. Wherever she goes when she's drifting, I trust it's a happy scene she's flying over.

Duty calls so I'd better be off and say "cheerio for now."

51. Bang, Bang, Bang

It's 5.00am. Mum is pounding on my door. She's already been up and opened all the curtains and is now demanding the butler. 'Honestly, she really cannot find decent staff these days' I laugh to myself.

I open the door and ask Mum politely, "What does it say on the door?"

Mum replies, quick as a flash, "It says Martin sleeping... what does it say on your watch?"

I laugh inside at the razor-like sharpness of her Bootle wit at this early hour and quickly get dressed to start the day at this newly designated getting-up time.

As it transpired, Mum didn't need or want anything. No doubt though, this won't be the last time she tries this new game! 'Butlers Door' like whack-a-mole only instead of a mole you get a sleepy butler popping his head round the door.

I bring her another cup of tea. She naps. I bring her cornflakes. She eats these and naps some more. I bring her another cup of tea. She naps again.

Meanwhile, my butler's brain is eager not to squander these extra chunks of time, so I set to and make a start on today's 'little project' – pickled red cabbage. I'm just gathering all the ingredients when Mum appears at the kitchen door. She's looking to see if someone was coming down the path.

"The bin's gone," Mum observes, as she opens the front door for a gander.

"It's there at the front Mum," I reply, pointing out of the front window.

"What's it doing out there?" she asks, looking increasingly confused by this strange weekly event.

"It's out early as we don't know what time the bin men are coming," I say.

Mum looks at me, then the bin, then at me again.

"I've never heard anything so daft in all my life," she says.

"Another cup of tea Mum?" I ask, seeing if the magic words will magically do their magic.

"Ooh, I'll say," she replies and off she shuffles, leaving me to do some more butlering.

With Mum sat enjoying another cup of tea, which is more of a comfort than it is an actual drink as such, I continue to set out the ingredients. Vinegar, cloves, salt, sugar, spices, coriander seeds, 'All present and correct Sir!' say the ingredients, all lined up ready for inspection.

The weighing scales have sat at the back of the kitchen cupboard for years, untouched and unloved. I decided to give them a thorough clean before I start and get them all sparkling and new looking before they're brought back into active service once more to weigh out the sugar and the salt.

The jars are cleaned and sterilised ready. Red cabbage is cored and quartered, chopped, salted and popped into the fridge in an old serving dish until tomorrow. The vinegar and other ingredients are warmed in a pan to dissolve the sugar, then covered and also left until tomorrow.

Now the whole house smells of warm vinegar. It reminds me of a time when Dad took us to a fish and chip shop on a rainy day in Blackpool.

The blue and white tiled walls had pictures of fish on them, in a dado like a frieze, all the way around the café. All the old folks used to wear macs or gabardines in those days and fish and chips used to get wrapped up either in the white unprinted paper, then in a layer of newsprint, or served hot on a plate if you were lucky enough to be 'dining in' that day.

I check on Mum briefly in the lounge and she's nodded off. I borrow the keys to the time machine and head back to Blackpool, circa 1970.

'Thinly sliced bread and butter, cut into triangles, on a powder blue plate; matching blue cups and saucers and a pot of tea for Mum and Dad. Dandelion and burdock for my brother and me in little glasses. It feels like we're the luckiest people in Blackpool, we're in from the rain and people are filing in and there's no other tables or seats left.

The café is filled with sounds… the metallic tap, tap, tapping of the wire basket holding the freshly cooked fish and chips, the roaring sound like an audience applauding as the cold, wet ingredients go into the boiling hot fat. The sliding of the glass doors on the warming section, the noise of the chip cutting machine in the back room chopping its way through steel buckets full of peeled potatoes. The hustle and bustle of folks coming in from the rain, of fish and chips being wrapped ready for eating out in bus shelters and covered doorways. The chatter of however many people all at once, like a cacophony of muted seaside conversations.

Then the meals arrive, the waitress in her 'pinny' balancing the same make of powder blue plates, battered fish hanging over the edges of the plates, perfectly cooked chips and a dollop of mushy peas. Slosh, slosh, slosh goes the vinegar as we all take a turn, salt on the chips, pepper on the peas. The chinking of china as Mum pours the tea for Dad and herself.'

Meanwhile, back in the here and now, Mum calls from the lounge, "Fred?" and the time-bubble pops, I quickly put the keys to the time machine back on the kitchen worktop and head back into the lounge to see what's required to warrant the call.

"Have you seen those birds?" Mum asks, as a jackdaw pecks at the suet balls hanging on the bird feeder.

And, as they say in moments such as these… 'all was right with the world'.

Right, I'd better get on with the to-do list!

Update on the day: just about to follow the ambulance to hospital. Mum fell and broke her hip. Will keep you posted!!

52. Chocolate Heaven

Mum's in hospital, she's had a successful operation to fix her broken hip. Her eyes light up when she sees me produce the strangely familiar purple bar. I break off a line, 'clunk' through the foil, then reach over the hospital bedside table and hand her a piece.

She places a single segment of chocolate on to her tongue. Her eyes close and she falls into what can only be described as chocolate heaven.

Cadbury's Dairy Milk, in its regal purple foil and distinctive packaging, has been Mum's favourite for ever. It's one of those fortunate items that has somehow escaped the rejection at the passport control of her fading memory. If Dad were here today he'd probably blame it on 'the power of advertising'.

Mum is sat in her hospital chair. In front of her is a table on wheels, its legs designed, I guess, to tuck under the bed, but also make sitting at it slightly challenging for some, Mum included, especially with her fragile legs.

On the table the familiar strand line of accumulated items is growing, tangled up with seaweed, fishing line and unwanted plastics, just like it did when Mum was at home. Of course, it's not seaweed et al, it's magazines, books, pieces of tissue, a hairbrush, cards, chocolate wrapper, drinks and whatever she's reading when I arrive.

I make a futile attempt at tidying a space only to drop a pen over the side that somehow gets lost amongst the paraphernalia of the hospital bed, the complicated table and the tubes and wires needed to sustain Mum when she gets low on fluids or food.

It's a battle to retrieve the pen, but I'd brought it so Mum could attempt her little pocket crossword book that she used to munch her way through like a crossword machine. I use a rubber-ended crutch to reach the pen from behind the bed wheel and feel myself getting flustered by the awkwardness of the manoeuvre. I feel the disapproving 'tuts' of the ladies in the other beds.

With the pen retrieved, we get to the crossword book and Mum opens the first page. Rather than diving to the crosswords, she attempts to read the introduction page, then the publisher's notes, wondering perhaps what the book is.

The first few crosswords are already filled in, possibly by one of Mum's carers at home. She reads these filled-in ones first, her brain not registering that the clues have already been answered, we plough on.

"My brain's not working," Mum says, frustrated with herself but equally accepting, it seems, of the things she deems suitable for the 'too hard pile'.

I hand Mum a card to sign for her grandson's birthday. She delights in the occasion and duly starts to write her love and best wishes, not really knowing who she's writing from anymore, just writing what comes to her in the best hand she can muster.

I hand her the envelope for the fully authentic 'card from Nana' treatment, and she writes another line of well wishes across the width of the envelope, her once neat handwriting now flowing more like a gesture than written words, but the love is ever present and that's all that really matters.

I spoke with the occupational therapist yesterday and they want me to see if I can coax Mum from her chair. They'd already tried every technique known to man to get her to take medicines, get up to walk, eat her meals, drink her vitamin drinks with all too little success it seems.

Fingers crossed, my coaxing will work. Until then, I've learned that Mum has been surviving on little more than the occasional piece of chocolate, which explains her '*Ice Cold in Alex*' moment earlier with the chocolate.

In my mind's ear I can hear an old Music Hall comedian saying, "Have you been?" I don't know who it was but we always used to say it to each other as a family when we were growing up. I say it again to Mum. She laughs. The nurse is walking past, she's in earshot too and shakes her head to say 'no she hasn't'.

The good news is that they have medicines for such things and hopefully quick enough reactions to assist as required when said medicines kick in!

We don't know yet how long Mum will be in this trauma ward for, but at least she is walking, albeit with the use of a frame and a nurse or two for stability. With good luck and a fair wind she'll set sail in a week or so, to carry her to a respite home before returning to her house and a resumption of this next chapter.

Anyway, she's in safe hands and with a little coaxing all will be well. Whatever happens, I'll keep you posted!

53. The Assessment

I arrived on the ward today to meet with the occupational therapist and discuss Mum's ongoing recovery and likely needs once she's discharged from the hospital.

I've always valued being punctual, so arrive a good ten minutes early, it's still lunchtime for the team so I'm invited to go and sit with Mum while the clock ticks steadily towards 1.00pm.

On entering Mum's side ward, she sees me approaching and immediately downs tools. My timing could have been better I think to myself, if I'd been ten minutes later she would have maybe finished more of her meal. As it was, seeing me put the mockers on the chicken and vegetable pie.

Mum greets me with the usual "Where have you been?" mixed with relief and delight for the familiarity of my presence as her brother, husband or son. Whoever I am today it's fine, as long as she's as happy as can be expected, that's all that matters.

I coax Mum to try a bit more of her meal while I make a start on the 'Jenga' pile of 'stuff' that's emerged on the other end of her side table.

Precariously balanced, like a seaside arcade penny falls machine, is a purple plastic folder filled with maps and memories from Liverpool I'd brought for her stay in the trauma ward upstairs. Above this is a pile of magazines, some old, some new, then two smaller piles above of A5 size books and crossword puzzlers.

Mum watches me attempt to balance all this, along with the packets of part opened biscuits, Cadbury's Dairy Milk and odd packets of jam, cleansing wipes, interleaved tissues and a hairbrush. She says, "I don't know who all that belongs to, but it's not mine!"

I carry on tidying and attempting to turn what looked like Einstein's desk into something a tad more minimalist and possibly less risky when it comes to manoeuvring the side table on its wheels.

The tea trolley arrives. In the old days these trolleys, complete with tea urn, used to be pushed by a lady with a headscarf. Nowadays, with equal opportunities and all that, it's a man who's about my age but at least he knows the drill, black tea in Mum's cup from home. Good man! I think to myself, Mum's got him well trained already.

Apparently, there were a few crossed wires and Mum's meal had been served at the wrong time, this meant putting back the mobility assessment until Mum had at least tried something off her red tray

ANOTHER CUP OF TEA

(the red tray being what they serve meals on for patients who may require some assistance).

By this time, Mum's table is starting to look like Kim and Aggie have done her a complete table makeover. The precariously piled clutter now replaced with tidy piles of clutter, the bits and bobs removed and the risk of things falling off now minimised.

Any good psychologist reading this will instantly recognise my affliction for tidying as symptomatic with my need to at least grasp on to control of one tiny part of my life right now. "Yes, his life was in utter chaos at this point, but at least he could put his hands on a ball of string or a pair of scissors once he'd got everything ship-shape!" says an imaginary friend reading a light-hearted account of my circumstances.

Meanwhile, Mum's meal had gone stone cold and with a little coaxing she made a start on the semi-warm rice pudding. This was met with a sparkly eye of recognition and a licking of the lips as she ate her way through the whole bowl, even scraping the very last of the pudding off the sides of the bowl.

The occupational therapist tries again some 20 minutes or so later. With him, possibly for backup, is the physiotherapist who's in charge of coaxing. If you can picture someone trying to pull a horse to the water and the horse staying exactly where it was, that's kind of what was about to happen again today, just like it had happened yesterday when they tried.

Today though they had me, their secret coaxing weapon. "Now then Joan, can you show Martin how you get up from this chair?" she tried, and Mum looked at me, did a 'tut,' then made a move for the walking frame. Up she stood, every sinew straining under the effort.

The next exercise was to get Mum to sit on the bed, then lie down, then get herself up out of bed. This must have taken what seemed like 30 minutes, poor Mum didn't have the energy to lift herself one way or the other.

Eventually though, with the aid of a bedside leverage contraption designed by Heath Robinson himself, she got herself vertical once more and was able to walk from her bed, the equivalent of the distance from the lounge to the bedroom.

In one sense it's miraculous that she's up and walking at all; in another sense with every fibre of her being she just wants to sit down and watch the world go by. She made the effort for me and I'm utterly humbled by her tenacity.

I'm also relieved that she didn't get violent with the physiotherapist who was at one point in danger of getting a 'knuckle butty' as she attempted to coax Mum off the bed. Still, it all went well and she avoided the full 'Bootle black eye'.

The occupational therapist is coming to visit Mum's house next week to assess what's needed and where to help Mum with her mobility.

Meanwhile, before I left I sneaked Mum another piece of Cadbury's Dairy Milk. Her eyes sparkled again. Mum's inner child said thank you, silently.

As a famous butler once said, "I'll be leaving you now Sir, Madam."

And so, I shall, with the promise of an update again soon.

54. Reality Check

Mum greets me with her usual bundle of emotions, a harvest festival basketful of relief, bewilderment, confusion, frustration and unconditional love. She's tucked up in bed, covered with a crisp white sheet and a pale blue towel over her.

The nurses struggled to weigh her today, her weight has been dropping steadily since she arrived and she's down to 38kg now, even the machine the nurses use said how underweight this is. They even have to keep her hydrated with a drip feeder.

My brother spoke with the social worker today, the one who'd been assigned to Mum to look into her continued care. The criteria bar must be set to some unfathomably high level, as Mum didn't qualify for any help!

I did my best to put a brave face on as I sat with her tonight, doing the crossword while my mind ran away with itself thinking unwelcome thoughts of the state of our country and the crazy politics that result in this inhuman response to our elders in their hour of need.

If ever I had a case of cognitive dissonance, this was it, on the one hand delighted by the care Mum has received during her stay, then on the other hand seeing how many professionals it takes to care for her only to be told, sorry, you're on your own now.

Mum needed the loo while I was there, so I called for a nurse to help her out of bed as she couldn't get herself up or out of it. It took him, a trained nurse, 15 minutes to help her out of bed, on to the commode, put a fresh nappy on then back into bed.

So here's Mum, I'm thinking to myself, seven years into her journey with vascular dementia, she's four weeks into what was supposed to be a six to eight week recovery, she can only walk with assistance, can't get in or out of bed, refuses food due to her illness, refuses to cooperate, is prone to UTIs (Urinary Tract Infections) and the subsequent delirium, and the grim reality is she's become just another number in an accounting office somewhere.

Mum is just one of 850,000 people with dementia in the UK. The numbers are set to rise to over one million by 2025 and climb to two million by 2051. I've got no answers, just sadness at the fact that so many of Mum's generation paid in all their lives for a National Health Service.

The NHS Mum and Dad paid into all these years was born out of the ideal that good healthcare should be available to all, regardless of wealth.

When it was launched by Nye Bevan on 5th July 1948, it had at its heart three core principles: that it meet the needs of everyone, that it be free at the point of delivery, and that it be based on clinical need, not ability to pay.

Obviously, when Mum eventually gets home we'll carry on as long as we can. The butler will resume his duties as best as he can and we'll make M' Ladyship's stay as comfortable as possible.

Luckily I've got a good imagination, so I'll just have to imagine there's a small army of nursing staff with me, you know, just like the ones who've been looking after Mum since the 14th May.

Anyway, I've thought of a solution. I'll dig out Mum's dreaded RED JUMPER, get her into a wheelchair somehow and take her to see the Health Secretary and I'll set Mum on him until he actually cries. That should shake things up!

Sod's law being what it is, today Mum was due to leave hospital, she fell on the ward and broke her other hip!

Ah well, he said with a deep sigh!

55. Fragments

The decline in Mum's overall health is noticeable. The effects of two falls, two broken hips, two operations and what will be more than two months away from her favourite chair accumulate and swirl around her like leaves caught up in an eddy in the brook.

Fragments of thoughts glide through her consciousness, she speaks out in her usual whispers but the content's all jumbled up and disjointed from the shared now. In one such instance she says, "I do hope Aunty Marion and Uncle Bill don't come tonight," frowning questioningly, with that worried look on her face that tells its own myriad of stories.

Sadly, Uncle Bill actually died in the 1970s and Aunty Marion remarried to Uncle Arthur. They're both long gone now and dearly missed.

"It's too far for them to come tonight Mum," I reassure her as they'd have to come from heaven via Liverpool and you know what the traffic's like (I think to myself, imagining we're in some old-fashioned sitcom).

Mum hasn't eaten her meal again, she's hardly drunk much either. Obviously they don't allow butlers to work here, but the regime of keeping Mum's cups of tea coming to her from dawn until dusk at least kept her hydrated.

Here in hospital, and thanks no doubt to numerous cuts, they've done away with actual butlers and replaced them with an intravenous drip via a cannula, which is somewhat lacking in the conversation department and quite painful to boot!

In spite of her declining health, Mum's still a keen observer of all the comings and goings, her eyes following the nurse as she tends to the other patients, questions arising after every word that's spoken to someone else, or watching all the comings and goings at the front desk, the ward's mission control.

Mum extracts her arm out from under the covers to have another look at her bruising. She's been in bed this afternoon and this evening, although she was up and in a chair this morning apparently.

It's been another laundry day at Mum's house today, the weather's been good so everything's had a nice dry outside on the line. There's a fresh supply of clothes in her locker and hopefully enough to squeeze some dignity out of the situation.

I'm holding her hand as she reads the writing she can see from her bed on various dispensers and signs around the ward. She looks at me, trying to see if I'm my Dad, or myself, she opts for the former and suggests, "We've had a good innings you and me haven't we?"

"We have Mum," I reply truthfully, as I've noticed over times like these that Mum's grasp of 'who's who' is momentary, as though she's looking through a kaleidoscope at a constantly changing scene.

Weight-wise, if Mum was down to below 38kg a week before she fell for the second time, the lack of food and fluids will mean she weighs even less now. Her tiny frame suggests it to be the case and short of whisking Mum home for a few meals with the butler, her inclination in here is to go without, so her decline is inevitable.

Yesterday I saw what a struggle it is for the nurses to help patients to do things for themselves. Mum wanted the loo but couldn't easily get up and go, so two nurses came and encouraged her to stand up under her own steam, then to get into a wheelchair.

Mum was also refusing her painkillers so the pain she was in was noticeable. Some while later, with lots of patience and encouragement, Mum got herself up and with a considerable team effort got into the wheelchair.

Seeing Mum so vulnerable like this, so physically weak now and struggling with everything apart from watching the world go by, I do wonder where on earth she'll find the energy to ever make it home. All we can do is take it one day at a time and make the most of these fragments of time we've been allotted somehow.

It's getting late now, the last drips of sun are disappearing and so I'd better bring the last of the washing in.

56. Remains of a Day

Well as you may have guessed, this has nothing to do with the book or the film *The Remains of the Day*… it does however still have a butler in it and in this case, a Lady rather than a Lord Darlington.

The story begins where the dutiful butler is visiting Her Ladyship in hospital and he arrives to find her slumped over in her high-backed armchair.

Also in a nod to the book, where the butler has regrets, in this scene he's regretting being away for a couple of weeks on holiday and finding her slumped over, fast asleep, seemingly unattended to, at least not in a manner she'd become accustomed to.

Black tea served in a spill-safe plastic beaker with a bendy plastic drinking straw wasn't quite how he imagined things would be. Whatever happened to her fine bone china teacup or the custard creams for that matter? The prerequisites for Her Ladyship's sustenance.

The lady in the bed opposite offered her valued inputs on the butler's arrival, the length of time Her Ladyship had been asleep, his name in case he'd forgotten, left with her for safe keeping by his brother the day before.

From across the ward she attempted to awaken her fully slumped companion in this place of rest and rehabilitation. The butler was happy to wait for the awakening to happen naturally and suggested politely that they let her sleep for now as she was probably still recovering from her lunch.

On the wheeled table by her chair side, a list of the à la carte menu lay at a neat diagonal, today's choices ticked but clearly not by Mum herself as they even included ice cream, something she's never eaten as she used to say, "I like it but it doesn't like me."

On the floor, more remains, in this instance broccoli from lunch perhaps, trodden in beneath her hospital issue grippy slipper-socks. On her lap, a lightweight hospital blanket to cover her pyjama bottoms. On her top, a nice summery blouse he'd brought for her before he went away.

He sat there for at least half an hour before she began to stir. Her head lifted, ever so slowly, her eyes opened and she looked around her to see if she'd arrived back in her favourite chair.

Her first thought was sadly a worried continuation of whatever she'd been dreaming and her waking words made no sense to anyone apart from whoever had been in the dream with her.

"Oh Martin," she eventually managed, as the pieces of the moment fell back together sufficiently for her to guess where she was.

As this was his first visit for two weeks, he came with a small bar of Dairy Milk Chocolate from the vending machine up the corridor. He pointed to the chocolate and offered to break a piece off as a 'welcome back to the current reality' gift.

"Ooh, yes please!" she replied, just as a child would when a rarely removed chocolate decoration off a Christmas tree is offered as an extra-special treat.

The expression of chocolate ecstasy is enough to indicate that it was just what the doctor had ordered, even though they hadn't and it was in fact just one more of the little idiosyncrasies that remained from their previous world before the falls.

Warm tea from the beaker was offered. She took a small sip then placed it back on the table, partly put off by the taste and possibly equally by the unrefined nature of the drinking vessel.

It was at this point where she suggested that the 'spending of a penny' might be a good idea. He checked her for wires and tubes in case she was still 'plumbed in' so to speak, where the need to get up is replaced with a need to remember how to do such things.

He got up and found a nurse. Apparently it normally takes two nurses to escort her to the lavatory, sadly the cuts had even reached this ward and rather than a walk with a frame, a challenging manoeuvre into a wheelchair was required.

Watching her struggle to coordinate the movement of her legs and feet to reach first the walker then the wheelchair reminded him just how far her health had declined. The lady who would often zip from the parlour to the conservatory or the kitchen to the dining room in lightning speed was now reduced to less than a shuffle that in turn took all of her energy to muster.

Again regretfully, the butler could see that his days of service are nearly over. All that remains of this day, this perpetual day that they shared for the past year at least, are the empty rooms where she once lived out her last year at home and the memories of all the comings and goings this entailed.

Perhaps there will need to be an advert placed in *The Times*, seeking a final butler's post before he hangs up his hat and white gloves.

As for Her Ladyship, she will eventually move from the ward to a more suitable home where nurses provide the essential personal care that a butler can't as it crosses long-established demarcation lines.

The house will be sold to pay for the care required. The contents auctioned off in a grand marquee on the lawns, or more likely given to charity or sold to a rogue who suffers from sharp intakes of breath at each valuation he's invited to give.

And the book? The story of this year of loyal service and unexpected happenings? Who knows? There may be more pages to add yet.

All we can say for certain is that the butler has one more regret, a regret about what's happened to the country's social care system where fine upstanding people who've paid into the pot all their lives are reduced to selling their homes to pay for the end of life care they'd always believed would be a given.

Until the next poignant, heartbreaking, laughter provoking page…

The butler signs off with a customary 'good evening' one and all.

57. The Postcard

Mum tries for the third time to read the postcard and make the mental connection between the fact that it's from me and more confusingly that I'm sat with her.

"Your post has arrived," Mum says, thinking perhaps that I've sent a card to myself just to test the postal system. She takes a couple of sips of warm tea from her plastic beaker, grimaces at the taste, then begins to read the postcard I've now handed back to her again.

I'd posted it last week and got notice, just in the nick of time, that she may be moving downstairs in hospital rather than to an intermediary respite home. With it being initially addressed to 'Ward 10', then with a 'or Ward 11' added after the event, in case it got delayed in the hospital system.

'At least she's sat up in her chair' I thought and the lady opposite gives me the news headlines of Mum's earlier battles with the nurses as they'd left her too long in bed apparently. In truth, there is no 'too long or too little', the illness just creates symptomatic behaviour that's as changeable as the weather.

As Dad would say, "You can't do right for doing wrong."

Mum reads the card over and over, labouring at times on the ward change on an otherwise error-free card, neatly written, well as neat as I could make it, properly addressed and even with its stamp on straight. I'm half expecting marks out of ten at this point.

A good five minutes pass by, I can hear an imaginary clock ticking loudly like on a TV quiz show and the ticks getting louder as Mum scans once more for errors. All is OK though and she places the card, without comment, back on her side table.

I tell her about the chores, ask her about her morning, check if there's anything needed and try my best to be heard without attracting security. Nurses come and go, a little girl of maybe 12 months old keeps running across the ward, bringing smiles to everyone.

Mum takes another sip of tea, grimaces again then declares she's just got to nip to the loo.

"Wait there a minute Mum," I say, Mum already trying to get herself up, not realising the pain involved or the jelly-like feeling of standing on just-repaired joints.

I get a nurse, who comes single-handed this time and grabs the walking frame. Clearly a different level of confidence from yesterday's nurse and no mucking about to be tolerated it appears. Mum gives her short shrift in reply and were it not for the age difference, if this was Bootle right now there'd be a fight for sure with knuckle butties and Kirkby kisses and everything!

Single-handed, the brave nurse attempts to escort Mum, under her own steam, still fighting her corner, in the walker to the loo, just opposite her bed. Mum is confused, disorientated, struggling to put one foot in front of the other and to even coordinate the lifting of the walking frame in time with each deliberated step.

It struck me today, after hearing yesterday they were intending doing a capacity test on Mum, that she may actually end up being declared 'fit for work'! The very fact she can respond to some questions some of the time does not necessarily mean that she's capable of answering the same questions the same way tomorrow or even an hour later for that matter.

Last night as I sat with her as she drifted in and out of consciousness at 7.00pm, I wondered if she'd see the following morning. I've had this same reoccurring experience so many times now I've lost count.

But back to the loo. Ten minutes later the nurse is escorting Mum back the way she came, Mum now stopping at every distraction possible, from the young girl to passing nurses, the journey of maybe six strides looks such hard work I wish I could carry her back to her chair.

Fresh blouses tonight as it appears there's been food spilt on every item of clothing, from slippers to jumpers. Ah well, when I was a lad there probably wasn't anything I hadn't got mud on at some point either, so life goes full circle once more.

I'll also bring a china cup for Mum to drink her tea from. "Perhaps the Wedgewood or the Royal Doulton M' Lady?" I should ask, but doubtless she'll probably reply, "Anything is better than a plastic beaker!"

Anyway, must dash, one can't afford to keep M' Ladyship waiting.

58. Jam Butties

"I've brought you some jam butties Mum," I say as I arrive.

"I've been to Knotty Ash and got them from the jam butty mines," I add, to see if a smile is possible.

Mum smiles a half-smile, the kind you do when you're sat up at a party, it's way past your bedtime and you feel yourself drifting off but you're still fighting to keep involved in the conversation.

I'd already cleared it with the nurses earlier, it's OK to bring in food for Mum providing it's labelled and dated, which is duly done in this case: 'Jam Butties, Joan Dewhurst, 24/7/2019' the label says.

They're not my best jam butties it has to be said, I bought this small sliced loaf for Mum and I realised as I was making it a proper jam butty needs to be on thick sliced 'door stops' with lashings of hard butter and best strawberry jam to qualify for the title.

Still, like all things culinary, we learn by our mistakes. I've been watching what I eat so couldn't even do a taste test, so just going by appearance alone, I think the judges on *MasterChef* would be kicking me off the show on the strength of this performance.

Mum drifts in and out of consciousness, her eyes nearly closed, enough to drift but not enough to miss anything going on.

"What's that?" she asks, after someone sneezes.

"What's that?" she asks, when someone coughs.

"What's that?" she asks, when something gets dropped in the ward...

In each case I attempt to describe what the noise was, ideally without the description being so loud that it further disturbs the patient who coughed or the one who sneezed.

Mum is in bed, plumbed into the drip again as she'd hardly drank a drop or eaten a morsel all day. She had nibbled on the grapes I brought earlier and did then eat a single piece of chocolate, which sent her immediately to chocolate heaven.

Off she drifted again, I tried to tidy up a bit, otherwise sat there wondering how this next phase is going to pan out. The latest battle, on top of the recovery from the two consecutive hip operations, is a DVT (Deep Vein Thrombosis) in her leg. She's had two scans today, the second to determine if it had gone higher up her body.

Injections of blood-thinning drugs into her stomach are the order of the day now and will be for some time we believe. Mum's hands show the bruising from all the battles she's been having over recent days as a result of this new invasion into her space.

Last night's thunderstorm had a few patients worried I heard, goodness knows what Mum must have thought. For myself, sleeping at Mum's house, I was in a deep dream during the storm and thought the thunder and lightning were at sea and that I was in a cottage by the ocean, with the lightning flashing out on the distant horizon.

In my defence M' Lud I've slept in three different beds inside a week so there's no wonder I didn't know where I was when I awoke this morning.

All in all, considering the butler is now almost surplus to requirements, I've been in good spirits, cracking on with the clearing and organising process, sifting through the stuff to keep, the stuff to send to charity and the stuff to maybe sell.

The exercise of three miles a day walking to and from the car to the hospital has been a welcome addition to my routine, and in spite of the worn-out shoes and socks, the fresh air, come rain or shine, is always a good thing.

I did find it hard when I learned of Mum's need for daily injections though, something she's always hated and struggled with. In that sense I see her often as having regressed to childhood, so the thought of her fighting the nurses because she's frightened is a tough one to reconcile, or it could be if I didn't know how to reframe the situation and find the positives.

Perhaps the creation of the perfect jam butty is my next milestone to aim for. One that the late Ken Dodd would have been proud of. Which reminds me, Mum met Ken Dodd when he came to Poynton back in the late 70s or early 80s.

Anyway, once more I'm digressing for England, so TTFN it must be.

59. You Say Tomato

You say "Tomato" and Mum says, "I looked in the back of the book and it wasn't there."

I say, "Would you like a cup of tea?" Mum says, "I don't know what all these adverts are about," and duly opens the magazine she's been reading and tries to find a page she's seen but now can't find.

Visiting time conversations today have been like two people conversing in two alien languages, each response failing to reach any form of comprehension. Even if Mum did hear me, her answers were incoherent and quite disconnected from the moment.

The DVT in Mum's legs has resulted in her left leg being twice the size of the other and a dressed wound on the right leg is bleeding, or has bled then stopped.

In spite of the added confusion of being effectively incarcerated for two and a half months for a crime she didn't know she'd even committed, in the moments between the confusion Mum can still muster a smile. Albeit a part smile.

Clothes washed and dried on this scorching hot day, I managed to restock her wardrobe ready for tonight and tomorrow.

Food wise, the plate from home I brought the jam butties in on has now vanished into thin air, as did her flowery patterned washbag and one of her china cups.

Apparently, Mum enjoyed a fairly good weekend, eating a little and drinking a little more than usual. Today though, possibly sensing it's a Monday, she's back on 'refusals' which is simply a 'no' to medicines, a 'no' to most food and a 'no' to most drinks.

She does still have her sweet tooth and ate a chocolate-coated ice cream from one of the neighbouring patients. It's interesting as Mum and ice cream have never got along before, well, all throughout my life anyway. I guess the dementia has selectively robbed her of the memory of not liking certain foods.

She did finish all her milk chocolate mini bars too which was quite some going. Whilst it's not the recommended nutritional intake for recovering patients, at least she's had something I guess.

When I came to visit earlier one of the nurses offered Mum a jam butty. Well she tried to offer it. Mum didn't hear the offer and only after I repeated the offer loud enough to hear it accepted down the corridor by a gent in another bedroom did Mum give me that funny look.

The funny look is generally when she's heard something you actually didn't say. Her mind reprocesses the word into something totally different and this merely compounds the confusion in any moment. I wonder if a writing pad may be the solution?

Anyway, as we know here in Britain, the answer to any problem is a nice cup of tea. I made Mum another cup of tea in the ward kitchen and duly delivered it as any self-respecting butler would in the circumstances. M' Lady duly responded with a "cheers… I think?" and here endeth another 'day in the life'.

It's set for rain tomorrow, which will probably mean more closed roads, even longer delays in getting to hospital and little chance of getting any outside jobs done. The upside though is a few nice refreshing walks in the rain from the car park to the hospital and back again.

Good job I packed a mackintosh!

60. Waking Dreams

Seeing me there, Mum smiles as she awakens from a dreamy sleep. Whether she's smiling at me as her son, the husband she's still mourning or her imaginary brother is immaterial, the main thing is she knows someone vaguely familiar is sat there with her.

Her eyes close again, comforted, yet as though the weight of her eyelids is too much and gravity is winning the fight.

The nurse arrives to see if Mum will take her medicines, all lined up in little plastic pots of coloured liquids. Two pinks that look like runny Angel Delight, two syringes and a clear liquid in another.

Mum never was keen on taking her medicine and tonight was no exception, the nurse even asked me if I'd persuade Mum to take them. I tried to no avail. Sleep was the much better alternative, so off she popped once more.

The nurse returned some time later and took away the medicines to be disposed of, another unchecked box on her report sheet. Mum drifted, her eyes closed, apart from one eye that was almost closed. She looked so peaceful so I just sat there at her side.

The ladies in the other beds gave me their updates and I could see from Mum's charts that she'd been up a few times in the night again, no wonder she's so tired.

Mum opens her eyes again, sees me and I assure her it's OK to sleep and I gesture as you do, with two hands together and rested against my head, as the spoken words just aren't landing today. Mum gets the 'charades clue' and closes her eyes once more.

As she lies there I think to myself how amazing it is that she's made it to 92 and how she would never have imagined reaching this age if you'd asked her 20 years ago.

The lady in the next bed mirrors Mum, both of them sleeping on their backs, both of them in pink hospital nightdresses, both of them a similar age. I recall then how much Mum loved the quiet times at home, where she could close her eyes and awake in the peace of her front room, even if it was to her a 'guest house,' at least it was a familiar one.

It's a comfortable silence we have, I love that, no need to fill any gaps, just the assurance that there's someone there with her. Wishful as it may be, I still hold on to the hope that when the long sleep arrives, whenever that may be, I'll be there with her.

During these past few months while I've been visiting Mum in hospital, I've watched the conkers growing on the horse chestnut near the park, they're almost ready for dropping now, maybe a week or so. If I'm lucky, I'll smuggle one in to show Mum, she used to always fill a little basket of them around this time of year.

And maybe I'll take my own trip in the time machine again tonight and head on back to 1968, playing conkers at home and at school. I'll see the conkers we collected in the park, all lined up on the kitchen windowsill, waiting to have a hole drilled through them with a twisted metal skewer that lived in the kitchen drawer.

Some conkers will be soaked in vinegar, all will have a string through the middle, a knot at one end and just the right length of string to avoid getting my knuckles bashed by Stephen who used to beat everyone at conkers, I recall.

If the Poynton floods had happened while we were kids, I bet we would have all gone out in wellington boots from Mr Hume's shop on Fountain Place and worn our dark grey duffle coats with tartan-lined hoods and wooden toggle fasteners that tucked into little loops on the front. We'd have probably filled our pockets with fir cones and conkers too if there were any to be found on the way!

Anyway, here's hoping the rain isn't too heavy tonight and the roads are passable from Poynton to the hospital tomorrow. We're meeting the doctors and consultants in the morning so hopefully we'll know more after that.

"Time for bed," said Zebedee!

61. What the Eye Don't See

"Oh, I do love you," Mum declares as I arrive on the ward.

Her arms are outstretched and otherwise she's all tucked up in bed. A number of nurses look to see who Mum's visitor is. I'm not rightly sure myself if truth be known. Perhaps I'm my father right now or Mum's imaginary brother or even myself for that matter. I hedge my bets hoping I'm me and attempt a hug over the restraining bars of her bed.

The ladies opposite are keen to fill me in on all the carryings on, the full menu of items eaten, medicines taken and the early morning call Mum gave them all by setting her alarm off at 6.00am just as the next team of nurses were starting their morning shift.

I'm envious, or in awe, of that amazing female trait of 'multi-conversational participation'. I'm keenly aware of my limitations as a male at one point as both ladies are speaking to me at the same time just as Mum's asking me a further series of questions about what they're saying.

The ladies possibly give me a 4/10 for answering sufficiently to them both but points were also potentially lost if I got the order of replies wrong, favouring one first and not the other when in fact the questions may have come in a different order. "Do keep up 007."

The ward, if not the entire hospital, is held together by women. Of course men play a part in the operations and general mechanics of the place but there's a whole other level of subtle communication going on that extends to the female patients and their visitors. At this point some of the male readers will be nodding along at how they too are amazed by the phenomenon.

I'm digressing. One of the ladies asks if Mum has anything to keep her shoulders warm and she's right as Mum is used to the near tropical heat of her lounge at home and here she is now, in just a couple of thin sheets and a nightie. I find her sky blue shawl and wrap it around her shoulders.

Mum recognises it and says, "Ooh, I've got one just like this at home!"

"This is the one from home," I say.

"You made it yourself didn't you Mum?" I add, proudly.

"I did... knit, knit, knit," she replies, reminding herself of all the hours she used to spend knitting in her favourite chair while Dad flicked from channel to channel with the TV remote.

"What have you been up to today?" Mum asks.

"I've been tidying cupboards today Mum," I reply.

"Oh well, you'll feel better after doing that," she says wisely.

Dad used to say, "What the eye don't see, the heart don't grieve about" and I hear him saying this as I'm sat with Mum, me bursting with a secret and Mum blissfully unaware that it was her cupboards I was tidying and her home I'm packing away into boxes and crates.

I spent almost the entire day stood at the kitchen sink, washing every cup, glass, plate, saucer, pan, serving dish, roasting tin, Tupperware box, casserole and item buried in numerous kitchen cupboards. It was like a spring clean only in this case it's a late summer one. Carol was here to help and she tackled the sideboard, the display cabinet and the itemising of literally hundreds of pieces. Now all neatly wrapped, boxed and listed ready for the next part of their own journey.

In the kitchen, once each cupboard had been emptied, they each got cleaned and polished to within an inch of their lives and restocked with the bare minimum to see us through until the house eventually gets sold.

Having rummaged around countless antique shops and car-boot sales over the years and worked for a homeless charity, I've a fair idea of how best to sort things ready for any eventuality. So, we now have crates filled with glass, crockery, pans, in-date food, earthenware, china etc, and each crate has its own manifest so we don't have to start unwrapping things to find them again.

We've set aside a small selection of treasured items to go with Mum to the nursing home – pictures, figurines, glass ornaments and the like – just enough to remind her of home but not so much that her space would be cluttered. The whole process is one of balancing... available time, objects, treasures and sensitivities.

Apparently there's a process called 'psychometry' where a person can sense the history of an object by touching it. I had that all day. Though in truth I was cheating as I already knew the history of most things I touched, apart from a few items that I hadn't seen before. I sure clocked up a few years on the old time machine today!

So many memories, a lifetime in fact, all laid out for a time, in neatly sorted piles. Piles of wicker-ware, piles of biscuit tins, piles of Tupperware, piles of books, piles of figurines and even piles of angels (Mum has them everywhere).

One of my favourite time-hops though came in the form of the old medicine bottles, the wonderfully evocative smells of TCP, witch hazel and liniments. These all whisked me back to Gran and Taid's house in Chester and the first time I'd opened the old wooden medicine cabinet on the wall.

Talking of Gran and Taid, one last thing came out from its hiding place that I thought had long gone. Gran's cap and gown, earned as a young lady in Bootle in the early 1920s and enabling her to become a music teacher before Mum was born. Somewhere amongst the old photos there's one of me wearing this cap and gown in their back garden in 1967 or so. I must find that photo again and join the dots up some day.

Anyway, time for some beauty sleep methinks and maybe another trip to times past!

62. Circular Conversations

Lady in the next bed: "Can somebody help me?"

Lady in the wheelchair: "I've been to help you, what do you want?"

Mum in her chair: "Pardon, what are they saying?"

Myself sat on Mum's bed: "It's the lady asking for help Mum."

Lady in the next bed: "Please can somebody help me?"

Lady in the wheelchair: "Go to sleep now."

Mum in her chair: "Pardon, what are they saying?"

Myself sat on Mum's bed: "It's the lady saying go to sleep Mum."

Lady in the next bed: "Can somebody help me get to sleep?"

Lady in the wheelchair: "Just close your eyes now."

Mum in her chair: "Pardon, what's that?"

Myself sat on Mum's bed: "It's the lady saying to close her eyes now."

Mum in her chair: "Who's saying that?"

Lady in the next bed: "Can someone help me to sleep?"

And so it's gone on all day since 8.00am apparently.

In Yorkshire they have an expression for someone 'calling out', they call it 'malling out', no doubt there are many words for it around the country. Whatever it's called, there's quite a lot of 'malling out' in here, I think to myself as I sit there observing the daily carry on.

Each time I walk past the first side room on the ward, a man 'malls out' "Please can someone help me," as though the request is triggered by any sign of movement outside his room.

In the next room to Mum's, a lady 'malled out' constantly the first time Mum was in rehab. It happened whenever she was left alone and I'd often hear her and wish I could just sit with her and quieten her troubled mind.

Tonight, there's a different 'malling out' from a guy a couple of rooms away. "Hoy," he shouts every so often, possibly imagining all kinds of things unseen to the rest of us.

After about 30 minutes it all goes quiet in Mum's circular conversation. The lady in the next bed has stopped calling for help every minute or so and Mum's sat quietly, nodding off in the newly found sliver of quiet in the noise of the day.

A visitor to the lady opposite has gone and sat with the lady in the next bed and is listening intently to her, chatting quietly and generally giving her someone to interact with. The quiet this provides is beautiful, I imagine how I'd be after 11 hours of these circular conversations, I'd be worn out no doubt.

I show Mum a photo on the iPhone. She holds it close up and recalls the times when she was young herself and I was maybe three years old. I'm trying to get her to do that thing that Dad used to do where I'd touch his mouth and he'd pretend to bite at my fingers with a SNAP and I'd pull my fingers away laughing at the thought of being bitten.

Mum asks me to show the picture on the phone to the other ladies on the ward, so I wander over with the photo and Mum sits there in her own space, glowing with the memories.

Someone's stolen Mum's blue knitted shawl today, the one she made herself all those years ago and the one bit of warmth and comfort she can wrap around her shoulders when it gets chilly.

Before I got here tonight Mum had been having a coughing fit and it worried everyone enough to call the doctor as Mum nearly passed out. It's happened a lot at home and I was used to comforting her while it cleared. Here though, they're taking extra precautions and may do an X-ray later to see if there's anything to see.

One of the downsides to this is that Mum's 'nil by mouth' so no cups of tea to quench her thirst or custard creams to nibble and make up for the meal she probably didn't eat.

Mum's own circular conversation continues throughout visiting time: "I don't know what I'm supposed to be waiting for?" or "Why do I need the doctor?"

Long story short, I had to get back home, so didn't see if the doctor came or not. I'll find out tomorrow. Fingers crossed Mum doesn't have any more coughing fits through the night.

Anyway, time for bed methinks.

63. Man in the Fan

"Does that look like a man to you?" asks Mum, straining her eyes to make out what's on the opposite side of the ward. "It does Mum!" I say to be agreeable.

It's a desk fan, next to the bed opposite and it's often set to oscillate. It's got a white surround and a black circle, so looks a little like a person wearing a fencing mask (as in the sport rather than the garden type).

Mum's sat in a nightie when I arrive, she must be half frozen given the kind of temperatures she used to endure in her lounge. I've brought with me the nearest thing to a shawl I could find. It's another one of Mum's creations, made by hand over countless evenings at home. I wrap it around her shoulders in an attempt to bring some warmth and comfort to the situation. Mum smiles at the outcome and recognises it as one of hers but only after asking if it's one I wear.

Another cup of tea and some custard creams add to the butler-like service. Mum tries to break a biscuit in half and instead it keeps breaking in smaller and smaller pieces, crumbs are everywhere and I'm reminded of the messes I must have got into with food when I was a toddler.

Mum gathers the crumbs on to the palm of her hand and proceeds to eat them one tiny sweet morsel at a time. It's a strange scene, knowing a loved one doesn't have long and yet is totally unaware of the circumstances she's in.

We chat in a kind of mother and son way, Mum asking unanswerable questions, me hoping my replies are the right ones and ones she can hear. Each moment feels like gold dust edged with precious gems. I revel in each moment, taking in everything, appreciating the time we have as though it's a last full day on what felt like an endless holiday.

I was just about to show Mum the picture of herself and me on the beach when the nurse came to apologise for the missing shawl. Apparently, it's been escalated up the chain of command so the powers that be are aware of its disappearance. There's no CCTV on the ward either for obvious reasons and so it appears that's the last we'll see of Mum's lovely comforter.

We get back to the photo and I mention that it could be Tenby, which Mum instantly agrees with. She then asks who the picture is of, as though her cognition is drifting from one moment to another, from lucid to distant and back again.

All the while I'm thinking of the gems I'd unearthed while clearing through cupboards and drawers, the little things that only have meaning to us, the funny things only we'd laugh at, the old things only we'd recognise.

I stop myself from talking about her home, or the one she'll be going to for that matter, we just occupy the present moment, drifting from any old topic to any old topic. And all the circular conversations we've had in this past year feel like treasures to replay and replay to keep the appreciation at the forefront of it all.

"Does that look like a man to you?" Mum asks once more for possibly the ninth time and I answer in agreement as though it's the very first time she'd asked. "It does Mum!" I reply and wish I could fly back in time, find Mum as she was and fly her back to see us talking now. Who knows, maybe that's what I'll do when she's left the physical realm, I'll just dream her back into being.

Mum's X-ray came back clear apparently so there's nothing to worry about on that front at least. She was diagnosed with COPD (Chronic Obstructive Pulmonary Disease) a few years ago, so who knows, the coughing could be related to that?

I mention to Mum about her X-ray results and she doesn't remember going for one or the coughing incident that led to needing one. If there's a list somewhere of final things that Mum's teaching me, then 'appreciating the moment' must be right up there as one of the important life lessons.

I left Mum with her favourite book, *Merseyside Tales* by Ken Pye; *Curious and Amazing True Stories from History*. Meanwhile, the 'Man in the Fan,' keeps turning his head from side to side and all's as right with the world as it can be.

64. Space Oddity

At this point, Mum's now been transported by space shuttle to a nursing home.

I'm back in Yorkshire.

It's 3.00am and I've just awoken from a dream of voids. I can hear David Bowie singing *Space Oddity* in my mind's ear.

I'm living 40 miles away from Mum now, it feels at times like it's 4,000 miles. It's funny that it's 40 miles away, we used to live 40 miles away from Mum's parents in Chester and no doubt she must have felt this same sense of distance from her Mum when her father died.

I visited Mum yesterday in her new nursing home. She slept all the way through my visit, unaware, at least visibly, that I was there, just as she had through my previous few visits to see her in hospital. I guess it's the sense of her drifting away from this life that awoke me, the myriad of thoughts that accompany such expected yet unknown things.

I digressed though from the 3.00am scene. Grief comes a'calling briefly, as he does, unannounced and uninvited. I tell him 'I'm not playing out right now', so he leaves with an oft-made promise to return once more when I least expect him.

In the semi-blackness of my room I lie there and think about big empty spaces, like the one I've felt of late as circumstances force us into new realities and alternative care arrangements.

I journey in my imagination to a few of the vast empty places I've been before, out on the sand banks at Red Wharf Bay, where the tents and caravans of St David's turn into little dots in the distance. Up on Kinder Scout where the village of Edale feels like a world away now you're here, high up on the heather-covered hills. Far out in the Sahara when we'd driven all day and not seen another living thing until we eventually spot a tiny shimmering light on the horizon, a refugee camp appearing like a mirage from the sun-baked desert.

Into each vast empty space I wander to, Mum is there, a tiny spec in the distance, still waving, still present, just too far away to reach, too far away to hear. And in these voids, where there's no choice other than acceptance, everything tangible seems to lose its appeal, nothing real holds its once perceived value.

I remember back to being four years old and having the often-occurring dreams that used to wake me up in the night. Mum would come into my room and talk me back round, assure me that everything was OK and it was just a dream, then I'd fall back to sleep, unaware that I'd still be recalling those vivid dreams some 53 years later.

The clock ticks slower than usual, as it does in the wee small hours. Eventually though it's a new day and the waking thoughts disappear one by one.

Much of Mum's house is empty now, just the larger pieces of furniture, a few bits and bobs to sort through at weekends perhaps. A lifetime's work and generations of history handed down through time like batons in a relay race that carries on through the centuries.

Mum's room in the nursing home is a welcome change from the constant noise of the rehab ward. Wonderful as the nurses, staff and other patients were at hospital, I knew Mum just wanted some shush and a much 'quieter carry on' than was possible where she was.

The dressing table in her room has a few precious items that will remind her of home, some pictures wait by the side to be hung on the walls by the maintenance team. The room has a patio door leading out to a garden and the trees beyond. Down the corridor there's a communal lounge, a quiet place where folks just sit and rest away the time between waking, eating, visits and sleeping.

I'm hoping Mum will be awake for my next visit, awake enough to say, "Oh, where have you been?" and maybe to ask, "Am I to stay here for now or come home with you?"

If we're lucky, the two new shawls that my inspiring friend Kerry has so lovingly made for Mum and posted today will be there when I arrive and I'll be able to get a photo of her all snuggled up and cosy.

How long Mum has left, nobody knows. I do know she's been in a lot of pain since leaving hospital and they've only just managed to get her to take some painkillers. I also know it's been too painful for Mum to walk so she's mostly in her new chair or her bed it seems. Sleep appears to be highest on her agenda now too, so ever the practical idealist, I'll carry on dealing with 'this and that' as time goes by.

The empty vast expanses of this morning's waking dream have all contracted back into the eternal now. Visual, tangible reminders of our time together surround me, 40 miles away from Mum's last house. A picture here, a trinket there, an old Dutch tin of rubber bands gets put to good use tidying cables, the old writing desk I bought to use at Mum's house, now in its new home, its drawers filled with ordered contents, its very presence here a constant reminder of these irreplaceable days where I played the ever-present butler role to M' Ladyship in her time of great confusion.

David Bowie fades back into earshot…

"This is Major Tom to Ground Control,

I'm stepping through the door,

And I'm floating in a most peculiar way,

And the stars look very different today.

For here,

Am I sitting in a tin can,

Far above the world.

Planet Earth is blue,

And there's nothing I can do.

Though I'm past one hundred thousand miles,

I'm feeling very still."

And so we say farewell to this wonderful panorama!

65. Three Ladies

I walked up to see Mum last night. It's a nice stroll from her old house up to Hockley where she's staying now. The forecast said rain and it's rather warm in the waterproof jacket. By the time I'm walking home it's raining so 'all's well,' as they say.

Mum was sat in a comfy chair, looking lost. To her right are two other ladies, one not quite as lost as Mum and the other even less so. Across the room, two elderly gents, also lost, one possibly just as lost as Mum.

I remember getting lost once on the way back from a school sponsored walk around Lyme Park. One of the teachers realised I was missing, along with a couple of others, and drove up to High Lane to find us.

Mum's a different kind of lost though. Her hearing and cognition are refusing to work in unison, so what appears to be an inability to hear could also be an inability to comprehend what's being said or asked.

The surroundings are new. Gone are the medical paraphernalia of the hospital rehab ward, now replaced with a garden view, a TV on the wall and unknown people sat with her, dressed now in daytime clothes.

The circular conversations of the hospital ward... where one lady says one thing, then Mum asks, "What was that?" that leads to a repeat of something said followed by a third person joining in for the chorus… continue here too, as though very well rehearsed.

Nurses come and go, in and out of Mum's peripheral vision, now walking on carpets rather than lino, now in less of a rush perhaps, still not what she'd hoped for though as none are her sister, her husband or her sons.

I've pulled up a chair and introduced myself to Mum before sitting down. There's no recognition now, no "Oh where have you been?" or glinting sparkle in her eyes that always shone out in moments like these.

66. Resurrection

In the distance, as I enter the hallway to Mum's nursing home, I can hear this oh-so-familiar 'clink, clink, clinking' of a spoon on a bowl.

Can it really be? It can't be! Is that Mum?

I quickly scan the lounge where the residents sit much of the time. Then the dining area, full of residents, all sat around tables eating breakfast. At the far table, sat low in a wheelchair, her hair brushed and nice clean clothes on sits Mum, eating her porridge.

The clink, clink, clinking of the spoon on the side of her bowl continues after each slow, deliberate mouthful. And before each mouthful she inspects the spoon and the porridge there on it, in readiness and anticipation.

My dam bursts. Tears flood uncontrollably down my cheeks before I reach her. I'd become so used to seeing her sleeping and practising hard for the long sleep, to see her sat like this, alone at a breakfast table but enjoying her porridge, was such a welcome and unexpected surprise.

To compose myself before joining her, I fumble for the mobile phone and find the picture on screen of Mum aged six. I try my best to quickly pull on my 'stoic cloak', look all grown up and make my 'everything's normal and casual' approach.

"Where have you been?" Mum asks, as though I'd just been playing out and been a bit late getting back.

"I've been in Yorkshire Mum," I reply, then wishing I'd thought quicker and simply said 'at home'.

"Yorkshire?" Mum frowns, unable to recall why I'd even think of venturing that far without permission.

"I'm just doing some decorating Mum," I add, just to see if I can veer away from anything on the too confusing pile.

"Oh, lovely, anywhere I know?" Mum asks.

"Yes, your house Mum, just freshening up the paintwork," I say, hoping the words will land in the right order.

Mum continues with her porridge, possibly processing.

In front of her on the table is another cup of tea with milk, not the way she used to take it, but tea none the less; tea and porridge, washed and dressed, sat at a table – all adds up to a biblical-scale miracle to me.

A few more mouthfuls later, I reach for the phone and on it I find the photo of Mum aged six. I show it to Mum as she enjoys a bit more porridge. She smiles. I tell her it's her aged six and she smiles longingly. Clink, clink, clink goes the spoon on the bowl.

I show her the picture on my phone of me aged six, just by way of a 'that was you and this was me' moment and Mum's eyes light up, remembering the boy that somehow has something to do with this strange man sat with her for breakfast.

Mum jiggles around on her chair, the way six-year-olds are inclined to do when they want the loo.

"I could really do with the loo," says Mum, jiggling like she's bursting.

"I'll call the nurse Mum," I say and in a second or two I've caught the nurse's eye and she's coming over to Mum.

"Are you all right Joan?" she says, getting up good and close to Mum so she can hear.

"I'm fine thanks," says Mum, no longer jiggling.

"Would you like to go to the bathroom?" the nurse asks lovingly.

"I suppose I could," says Mum, jiggling again.

And off she trundles, her brain now holding only a few seconds worth of attention and looking like she's now wondering where she's being trundled off to!

I go to Mum's room to check on things. Her bed is made, everything's tidy, I open the window and can hear the melodic voices of the Liverpudlian decorators who were all chatting outside on their tea break. I wish for a moment Mum could hear them.

"They're proper Wackers," she'd say if they were able to come in and have a natter with Mum.

Anyway, this is only a flying visit as I'm conscious of distracting Mum from eating her breakfast. I say my goodbyes and leave her to finish her porridge in peace, remembering Gran and how she used to like her porridge with a pinch of salt.

I leave the nursing home dining area, for some reason still struggling to put on my 'stoic cloak' and head for the doors, overrun with a bucketful of unexpected emotions… amazed at Mum's resurrection, relieved at the fact she's actually eating something and genuinely humbled by the love the nurses show in their care for the residents.

In one of my favourite songs of the 1970s – 10cc – *I'm Not in Love* – I can hear Kathy's voice in the background saying, *"Be quiet, big boys don't cry, big boys don't cry."* Well, in some very rare circumstances we do, or at least I do and that's one of the ongoing struggles, how to cope with the constant yet unpredictable contrasts involved with dementia.

'Stoic cloak' back on, I swoop out of the nearest telephone-box-changing-kiosk, fly over the Hockley rooftops back into the village and arrive at Mum's house to crack on with the decorating.

Her home is now a house, bricks and mortar, paint and paper. Mum, Dad and all the memories of our lives together now neatly downloaded into the indelible back-up drive of my heart.

And so… "On, on," said Thomas the Tank Engine.

67. Lost and Found

Mum sits in a comfy chair. She's alone in the lounge of the nursing home. On her lap, the evidence of breakfasting crumbs. The other residents are in various stages of preparedness, some eating breakfast, some still in their rooms, otherwise, all is calm and peaceful.

In a rare moment of cognition, Mum recognises me and greets me with the customary open arms that would have Mike Tyson reaching for the Kleenex. I'm obviously delighted to see Mum with her inner light shining so bright and it feels like all my Christmases have arrived at once.

The first thing I notice as I sit down for a well-earned break from decorating is that Mum's wearing a new pair of glasses. Well, I say new, what I mean is someone else's glasses, as these are quite different from her own. Their shape and colour now etched on to my own memory from hunting for them so often.

I go to make Mum another cup of tea and ask the nurse in charge if she has any ideas on the whereabouts of Mum's glasses. It's a frequent thing, this losing of things, and must be a daily challenge for the staff as I'm sure the art of losing stuff is a gift that other residents have also honed to the highest of standards.

Sure enough, one of the male nurses recalls Mum having swapped glasses before, and he knew, just like I did, the exact shape, colour and size of Mum's glasses as he'd been the chief finder on more than a few occasions.

I left my cap with Mum while I went to make her tea and speak to the nurses. On my return there's Mum sat wearing my cap! What a moment, I fumble for my phone and capture a quick snap before the moment's lost.

And talking of lost, sitting with Mum I notice she's only got one ring on, the other two are missing. I check in her room and they're nowhere to be seen. Apparently when fingers get too small, rings are placed in envelopes and stored in the office safe. It must happen a lot.

Mum enjoys a few sips of her tea and begins to ask all kinds of unanswerable questions. For me this is like winding the clock back to before her fall, I nod along and reply in unfathomable answers to which Mum nods in appreciation of the snippets she gleans in return.

We talk about Mum's new shawl. I tell her about Kerry who made it and Mum says,

"Ooh, she must love knitting, she's done a wonderful job!" and I wish Kerry was here to take a bow and tell her all about how she came to make the shawls in the first place.

I show Mum some photos of the family and the one of her raising a glass at the Harrington Arms. "Oh gosh, don't I look old!" she says, still thankfully unable to recall her current age or circumstances for long enough for it to matter to her.

Mum drifts a few times, one eye beginning to close slowly as the room starts to fill with residents, one by one assuming their place for the spaceship ride to somewhere new. I wrestle the almost gone cup of tea from Mum's hand so it doesn't get spilt. The movement wakes her for a moment then her eyes begin to close once more and on her face a constant smile of knowingness.

Eventually she's off into a deep sleep, one eye partially open but not enough to spoil the slumbering. A radiant smile is still on her face.

It's a parental smile, one that says right now everything's all right with the world.

And thinking about parental smiles, I watch her sleeping, the way a parent watches a child sleeping. Mum's still Mum of course only now I've seen the picture of her aged six, I see the child sleeping within. It's another priceless moment to treasure.

Watery eyed, 'it must be the dust again', I wander off to get on with the decorating and leave Mum to her sweet dreams. I say sweet dreams and trust that's exactly what they are as the smile's still present as I take my leave.

I'll find out another time about the missing rings, but for now I've found an entirely greater treasure – Mum smiling.

Oh, PS, they found Mum's glasses, they were in Margaret's room!

68. Reflections

The curtains are partially opened. Mum's room is bathed softly in mid-morning sunlight. Lying awkwardly in and amongst a bundle of sheets and blankets is Mum, partly on her side, halfway on and halfway off her propped-up pillow. On the floor there's a pressure pad and a crash mat. On the bedside table that's positioned over her, a bowl of cornflakes and a beaker of orange juice.

The right-hand side of Mum's face is badly bruised, her left arm is heavily bandaged and I'm at a loss for the right thing to do or say. I just hold her hand and stand awkwardly myself in a bid to avoid standing on the pressure mat and setting off an alarm.

Mum fell late on Tuesday evening. She'd got up, fallen and banged her head and cut her arm. She was found unconscious and rushed to hospital. My brother followed the ambulance to Stepping Hill and kept me updated by text.

I'm staying at Mum's house and the phone rang at 2.30am. It took me a while to figure out where I was and which phone it was that was ringing. As it turned out the call was from the duty doctor at Stepping Hill and he thought he'd called the number for the nursing home. Establishing that I was her son, he suggested Mum would be discharged in the morning.

Mum was eventually discharged later in the day and returned to the nursing home and back to her room, now sadly in a very delirious state. I called to see her this morning in the possibly unrealistic hope that she'd be sat in the dining room having her breakfast.

Last week I sat with the former nurse who's got the thankless task of telling families that their loved one isn't covered for CHC funding (Continued Health Care). The social worker who joined us told us of how her own relative failed to meet the criteria for funding. I came to the conclusion that it's probably more likely that you'd win the lottery than qualify for CHC funding.

The upshot of the meeting was that (off the record) there isn't enough money in the NHS to cover the care costs of the country's aging population. Therefore it's down to each of us to save up for our own care in old age rather than to expect to leave anything resembling an asset for our children or remaining family.

Thinking of the morality of the situation, or the potential lack of it for Mum and the 850,000 other sufferers of dementia in the UK right now, I guess it boils down to 'politics' and right now Nye Bevan's words are resonating through the valleys of time:

"I have never regarded politics as the arena of morals. It is the arena of interest."

Ho Hum

69. Eternal

As tough days go, that was a tough start and the day had hardly begun.

Mum is sat precariously in a wheelchair at the breakfast table, her eyes unable to stay open for more than a few moments at a time.

The dining room is full of residents having their breakfast and staff going from table to table like worker bees making sure everyone has something resembling a portion of normality.

In front of Mum is a bowl of gone cold porridge, a tepid cup of tea with milk, neatly set out on a paper doily. Mum opens her eyes for a moment and sees the edge of the doily, its delicate pattern reminding her perhaps of the drawer full of handmade ones she'd made over the years.

In a moment of her eyes being open I show her the photo of herself aged six. Mum looks but can't speak, the effort now almost beyond her grasp. She looks at me and tries to figure out if I'm one of the staff or someone she once knew.

She tries to speak but the words can't even gather themselves into a whisper. I get in close and put my ear in near as she tries again, but no words make their way out into the room. I sit back in my chair and see if I can lip-read the words she's wanting to share. She gives up and closes her eyes once more.

Her face is cut, bloody and bruised down the left side. Her left hand and wrist are badly cut and all roughly fastened together with butterfly stitches. She's been in bed for the past few days since the fall and this is her first day up and dressed.

Mum reaches out and her hand heads precariously towards the porridge so I shift this out of harm's way. She's reaching for a pager that's been left on her 'table for one'. Outside, in the garden, a pair of squirrels bob across the patio towards the trees. A tray of home-grown baby tomatoes sits on a tray by the window to ripen.

I reach out and hold Mum's hand. Her eyes open for a moment then close again as she drifts once more towards peaceful rest. It's an eternal moment, holding hands with Mum as she descends into sleep. It's also a challenge to hold a camera steady to capture the moment and wipe away the tears with my left hand.

The nurse arrives to administer Mum's daily injection. The fight's gone now, no more warding off all-comers, just compliance and an almost teenage expression of 'whatever'. Mum looks into the eyes of the nurse with the needle and gives another teenage expression 'like bothered loads,' she'd say if I could put words in her mouth like Johnny Morris used to do on *Animal Magic*.

A plate of toast and marmalade arrives.

"Ooh, your favourite Mum!" I say, encouragingly.

Mum just looks blankly into the space between us.

Unable to hold her head upright she drifts once more towards the peace of sleep.

I suggest to one of the nurses that Mum might be better off in a comfy chair, what with breakfast having been refused and her body's urge to slump forwards.

A male nurse fixes Mum's wheelchair ready for the ride to the lounge. It's only a few yards away so she's soon helped up from the wheelchair and into a comfy armchair for a proper, no-holds-barred 'sleep of sleeps'.

Another cup of tea is ordered and a little table slid in front of her for convenience.

Mum sits exactly like her six-year-old self would have sat at school, knees touching, hands by her side, head towards the blackboard (TV) and a look of someone doing their utmost to stay awake, but the fight is lost within moments and her eyes have closed once more.

My usual 'chipper' self is fighting his way out past the inevitable struggle of leaving Mum sleeping like this, unaware, at least consciously, that I've even been there and more importantly, unaware where she is or where all her loved ones have gone.

'Anyways,' he says. Stiff upper lip and all that. Back on with the decorating clobber, back out with the paint and the rollers, back up the ladders etc, etc.

This is the way it is right now and all we can do, as Churchill once famously said, is to "Keep buggering on!"

70. Love, Love, Love

Goes the famous Beatles song.

"Love is all you need."

This just happens to be one of the countless songs we played today in Mum's room as she set sail for distant shores unknown. Mum disappeared over the distant horizon at 4.55pm, my brother and I holding her hands, Carol sat with us and all the family up to speed and awaiting the news of her final voyage.

Mum kept me up all night last night, not deliberately of course, but in a spiritual sense as she visited me all through the night, filling my otherwise pitch-black bedroom with a light show like the Northern Lights. 11.30pm, 2.30am, 4.00am… I'd awake to these lights and all I could do was sit up in bed and talk to Mum in my head, which needless to say left me somewhat bog-eyed this morning.

At 8.15 this morning we got the call from the nursing home to say that Mum was at the end of her life and we drove straight over to Poynton from Yorkshire. Had the call come minutes later we'd already be heading north to Bradford to see Carol's Mum.

On the bedroom door to Mum's room a butterfly had been placed, possibly a sign to the staff that someone is about to fly away, a metaphor for a metamorphosis perhaps.

Rob and his wife Jan were already in Mum's room when we arrived and Welsh choir music was playing on the special 'dementia friendly' player Rob had set up in Mum's room to provide some musical background to Mum's last hours.

A few nights earlier Rob had been playing piano for the residents in Mum's lounge and a couple had even got up to dance, which in turn had made the nurse cry as it was such a transformative experience for them.

Rob and I grew up in a home full of music, from the classics through to Sinatra, from jazz through to pop. Mum had attended many of Rob's concerts around the country and beyond and every year he'd made Mum and Dad a tape or a CD of his piano medleys that were subsequently played and played and played.

Mum's last whispered words to me were, "I love you." The power of speech had already left her the day before but these words came through in lip-reading form, delivered with love upon seeing me watching over her.

The day was long. Her passing when it came, the most peaceful of affairs you could have ever have experienced. With Rob sat on a chair holding Mum's right hand, me sat on the edge of the bed holding her left with my other hand on her heart, her breathing faded slowly away until the thread she was holding on by reduced in width, through degrees of fineness, until it disappeared from view altogether.

A great wave of relief and emotion and appreciation washed over me as Mum's breathing quietly stopped and her spirit left her body. No more struggle, no more confusion or worry or pain, just liberation from this phase and arrival into the arms of all those who had gone before.

With all the fine details to be attended to over the coming days, Mum has now been whisked away to a place of rest and we're all back in our respective homes. Family notified and messages received from near and far, it's time now to reflect upon this wonderful legacy of love that Mum has left for us.

Thank you one and all for the love, guidance and encouragement you've shared with me over the course of this amazing journey.

To quote Mum on this most special of days ... "I Love You."

About the Author

Martin started work in 1979 as an apprentice in the reprographics industry, working on projects for brands like Rolls Royce, Bentley and Jaguar.

In 1989 he established a successful new business in the same field, then since 1999 he's been involved in a diverse range of projects from design and print consultancy through to humanitarian aid delivery in Africa.

More recently he's worked for a homeless charity, designing and implementing a system for the redistribution of surplus food to vulnerable communities.

He's a mentor and trustee for a UK military charity, a Fellow of the Royal Society for the Arts and Member of the Royal Photographic Society.